OPTION STRATEGIES

OPTION STRATEGIES

Profit-Making Techniques for
Stock, Stock Index, and
Commodity Options

Courtney Smith

JOHN WILEY & SONS

New York • Chichester • Brisbane • Toronto • Singapore

Library of Congress Cataloging-in-Publication Data

Smith, Courtney.
  Option strategies.

  Bibliography; p.
  Includes index.
  1. Financial futures.   2. Put and call
transactions.   I. Title.
HG6024.3.S55   1987   332.64'52   87-6174
ISBN 0-471-84367-9

Printed in the United States of America

10 9 8 7 6 5 4 3 2 1

Preface

Options are powerful tools and add new ways to adjust the risk and reward of trading. They allow investors and hedgers to create new ways to profit from market swings. No longer are investors locked into simply buying or selling a financial instrument. Now they can capitalize on such factors as changes in volatility and the passing of time.

Investors can now fine-tune their position to exactly fit their market perspective. Why take a big risk of buying an instrument when you are merely looking for a small rally? Use a bull spread instead! Do you think the market is going to drop for the next month, then rally? Use a calendar spread!

There are now options on most of the commonly traded financial instruments, including stocks, Treasury bonds, stock indexes, and futures.

I wanted to write this book to provide a map for option strategies. There are already several good books on options and options pricing, but they didn't satisfy the goal of providing a practical guide to option strategies for all instruments. For example, many books have sections on only the strategies that presume a bullish market stance. Bearish strategies have been largely ignored. Most options books do not provide much assistance in the selection of the proper strategy. Now that I am bearish, what is the best strategy? If the books talked about the proper strategy then they often didn't help select the right option. For example, you have decided that a bear spread will be the ideal strategy for your market outlook. Should you use puts or calls? Which strike prices? Which expiration month?

I also wanted to provide a guide to followup tactics. I'm in my bear spread and the market has rallied. What can I do to protect myself or to increase my profit potential?

I want this book to be a practical guide to option strategies that will be referred to many times. Wear it out.

                                                                        COURTNEY SMITH

New York, N.Y.
April, 1987

Contents

OPTION
STRATEGIES

1

Introduction

A. Decision structures
B. Simplification of options calculations
C. Outline of the book

Welcome to <u>Option Strategies</u>. This book will take you on a guided tour of the world of option strategies.

Options present the investor with a myriad of new strategies. Some are very conservative, such as covered call writing, while others are very speculative, such as naked call selling. Options provide more and often better ways to fine-tune your investing strategies to expected market conditions.

This book covers all types of options: stock index, stock, and commodity. Bullish and bearish strategies are covered equally. It will be useful to all options traders and hedgers, from novices to professionals. To this end, several features are introduced.

DECISION STRUCTURES

Decision structures are an ordered line of inquiry, consisting of a series of questions and answers that assist you in analyzing potential trades and in determining your action after you have entered a trade.

First you must determine your objectives. Identifying your objectives will help you achieve them. This self-evident truth is often forgotten. Two main questions can help isolate your objectives.

First, how much risk are you willing to take? The answer to this will guide your decisions. Each person has a subjective criterion of risk. You must have an idea of your level of risk so you will feel comfortable with your investments.

What kind of return do you need to take on that level of risk? The greater the risk, the greater should be your prospective reward. Look at competing investments. You may have found a low-risk covered write but the return may be just above Treasury bills. Why bother with such a trade? Look for those opportunities that have significantly more reward, though they also have more risk.

SIMPLIFICATION OF OPTIONS CALCULATIONS

Most discussions of options calculations are too simple. They highlight the important issues rather than present seemingly irrelevant information. However, in the final analysis, we do not live in a simplistic world. Reality is complex.

The major area of simplification has been in the mathematics of options. In general, the calculations given in books and articles have ignored such factors as transaction costs and carrying costs. In most cases, this is not critical. However, there is no need to invest in an option trade and lose money because of forgotten factors.

The discussions of risk and reward in the strategy chapters of this book focus on the strategy and usually do not mention the carrying charges, unless they tend to be a major determinant of profitability. For example, the decision to buy a call is rarely going to be affected by carrying charges, but an arbitrage between an underlying instrument and a reverse conversion is dominated by considerations of carrying charges.

Carrying charges must therefore always be considered when considering a strategy. Let's take a look at the various costs, including transaction costs, the bid/ask spread, slippage, and financing costs.

Transaction costs are an ever-present cost of trading. We use the term transaction costs to include commissions, the bid/ask spread, and slippage. Typically, the largest transaction cost is brokerage commissions. Brokerage houses charge commissions on all transactions. Many option strategies involve the use of options in conjunction with other instruments. For example, a covered call write program in stocks involves the sale of a call against the purchase of the underlying stock. The commission on the stock purchase and on the eventual sale should be considered in the investment decision.

Another potential transaction cost is the bid/ask spread of the investment. All options and related instruments have a bid/ask spread. For example, an option may have a last price of 4 1/4, but the bid may be 4 1/8 and the ask may be 4 3/8. The bid is the highest price that someone is willing to pay for the option, while the ask is the lowest price at which someone is offering to sell the option. In general, most investors will have to pay the ask to buy an option, and will sell at the bid price. This has the effect of inducing slippage in calculations of profits, risks, and break-evens. It is usually wise to include at least one minimum tick or price movement into the costs of your option trade. For example, bond futures options trade in units of 1/64. It would be a good idea to subtract 1/64 from your expected sale price and add 1/64 to your expected purchase price.

Slippage is the final transaction cost, and is related to the bid/ask spread. It is the difference between the price that you expect on the fill of an order and the actual cost. For example, you could expect to get a fill at 1 7/8 on a purchase of a call, but the market is active and volatile and your order is not filled until the market is up to 2 1/8. *Very* conservative investors should include at least another tick on the expected price as slippage for computing expected returns on a trade.

Carrying costs are often overlooked and/or idealized. Carrying charges represent the costs to carry an open position. Traders should at least consider the opportunity cost of initiation and carrying a particular trade. There are an infinite number of investment possibilites. When you decide to do an option trade, you have implicitly rejected all other investment possibilities. You have eliminated the *opportunity* to invest elsewhere. Traditionally, the opportunity cost has been quantified as the Treasury bill rate because it is considered riskless.

Leveraged positions have a finance charge. This finance charge must be considered before initiating a position and while calculating the possible outcomes. For example, a covered write against a stock bought on 50 percent margin will have the profit potential reduced by the financing charges. We will use the term *carrying charges* or *carrying costs* as a shorthand reference to the various costs associated with carrying a trade or position throughout this book.

OUTLINE OF THE BOOK

We will begin with two chapters that form a base for the remainder of the book. Chapter 2 - The Fundamentals Of Options gives the basics. Even experienced options traders should scan this chapter to make sure that we are all using the terminology in the same way. Chapter 3 - Selecting A Strategy outlines several of the considerations that are important in selecting a strategy. The remaining chapters discuss various strategies, the risks and rewards of the strategy, the selection of the various components of the strategy, and the necessary follow-up actions.

2

The Fundamentals
Of Options

This chapter will give you the basics of options. It is necessary to know this information before going on to the other chapters. The concepts presented here will be referred to throughout the book.

WHAT IS AN OPTION?

An option gives the buyer the right but not the obligation to buy or sell something. We will call that something the underlying instrument (UI). Throughout this book we will refer to the underlying instrument as a generic something, which could be a stock, like 100 shares of PaineWebber stock, something tangible, like 100 ounces of gold, or something conceptual, like a stock index. Conceptual underlying instruments call for the delivery of the cash value of the underlying instrument. For example, the popular S&P 100 option calls for the delivery of the cash value of the index. Also note that options on stocks call are for 100 shares of the underlying stock. Options on futures call are for the same quantity as the underlying futures contract.

An option traded on an exchange is standardized in every element except the price, which is negotiated between buyers and sellers. All aspects of over the counter (OTC) options are negotiable. The examples in this book assume exchange-traded options, but the analysis also applies to OTC options.

Options can be bought or sold. A person who has bought an option is long the option. A person who has sold an option is said to be short the option or to have written or granted the option.

There are two types of options: calls and puts. A call gives the buyer the right, but not the obligation, to buy the underlying instrument. A put gives the buyer the right, but not the obligation, to sell the underlying instrument. Call option buyers hope for higher prices and put option buyers hope for lower prices. Call option sellers hope for stable or declining prices and put option sellers hope for increasing or stable prices.

For every buyer there must be a seller. Selling a call means that you have sold the right, but not the obligation, for someone to buy something from you. Selling a put means that you have sold the right, but not the obligation, for someone to sell something to you. Note that the option seller has an obligation but no right. In exchange for this obligation, the seller receives a premium, which will be explained below. Other terms for selling are *writing* and *granting*.

The buyer of an option pays a premium to the seller. The premium, or price, is determined by the open market at the various exchanges. Option buyers pay the premium, while option sellers receive the premium. For example, you could buy an IBM April 140 call for a $5 premium. The buyer of the option pays the premium to the seller.

There are two types of transactions: opening and closing. An opening transaction initiates an options position, while a closing transaction liquidates the trade. An opening buy is followed by a closing sale or exercise (a closing exercise following an opening buy means that buyers avail themselves of the right that was bought). An opening sale, or write, is followed by a closing buy, or exercise (a closing exercise following an opening sale, or write, means that sellers must meet their obligation). This distinction is important for margin purposes.

The open interest is the total of open options contracts on an exchange, and is calculated by the exchange. Every option outstanding is counted. If you open buy an option, the open interest increases by one. Note that you cannot tell the number of buyers or sellers, only the number of contracts existing at the close of trading each day. The open interest is useful in determining the liquidity of an option. Liquidity tends to increase as open interest increases. High liquidity is important if you want to place large orders to buy or sell. Open interest is typically reported by the exchanges on the day following the particular trading day.

It is easy to understand the rationale of buying an option. You get most of the benefits of owning the underlying instrument without most of the risk. In one sense, buying an option can be compared to insurance. For example, insurance lets you have the benefits of owning a car, minus the cost of the insurance premium, without most of the risk of accidents. In options, the call buyer gets most of the price appreciation of the underlying instrument, if any, without the risk of prices moving lower. The put buyer gets most of the price depreciation, if any, without the risk of prices moving higher. The seller of the option takes the risk of price appreciation or depreciation in return for the premium, which is similar to the insurance premium.

Why would anyone want to sell options if they are not in the driver's seat? The answer is money. The price that option buyers must pay is set in an open market. If buyers don't bid high enough prices, sellers won't sell. The net effect is that options prices are bid to a level that option sellers believe compensates them for the risk of selling options. In effect, the buyers and sellers have exchanged an element of risk for a price.

An option can be liquidated in three ways: a closing buy or sell, abandonment, and exercising. Buying and selling are the most common methods of liquidation. Abandonment and exercise are detailed below.

EXERCISING OPTIONS

An option gives the right to buy or sell an underlying instrument at a set price. Call option owners can exercise their right to buy the underlying instrument and put option owners can exercise their right to sell the underlying instrument. The call option owner is calling away the underlying instrument when exercising the option. For example, owners of Oct ATT 50 calls can, at any time, exercise their right to buy 100 shares of ATT at $50 per share. The seller of the option is assigned an obligation to sell 100 shares of ATT at $50. After exercising a call, the buyer will own 100 shares of

ATT at $50 each, and the seller will have delivered 100 shares of ATT and received $50 each for them.

There are two styles of options: American and European. American options can be exercised any time before expiration, while European options can only be exercised at expiration. We assume American-style options throughout this book, except where mentioned.

Only holders of options can exercise. They may do so from any time after purchase of the option through to a specified time on the last trading day. For example, stock options can be exercised up until 8:00 p.m. (ET) on the last day of trading. Option owners exercise by notifying the exchange, usually through their broker. The writer of the option is then assigned the obligation to fulfill the obligations of the options.

Clearinghouses handle the exercising of options and act as the focal point for the process. If you want to exercise an option, you tell your brokerage house, which then notifies the clearinghouses. The clearing corporation assigns the obligation to a brokerage house that has a client that is short that particular option. That brokerage house then assigns the obligation to one of its clients that is short that particular option. The assignment is usually either random or first-in/first-out. However, the brokerage house can use another method if it is approved by the relevant exchange. It is therefore important for option writers to know their brokerage house rules on option assignment.

Once assigned, call option writers must deliver the underlying instrument or the equivalent in cash, if the contract specifications call for cash delivery. They may not buy back the option. They may honor the assignment of a call option by delivering the underlying instrument from their portfolio, buying it in the market and then delivering it, or by going short. The assignment of a put option may be honored by delivering a short instrument from their portfolio, selling short in the market and then delivering it, or by going long.

After exercising an option, you will be holding a new position. You will then be liable for the cost and margin rules of the new position. For example, if you exercise a long stock call and want to keep the shares, you will have to either pay the full value of the stock or margin it according to the rules of the Federal Reserve Board. Alternately, you could sell it right away and not post any money if done through a margin account. If you had tried to sell it through a cash account, you would have to post the full value of the stock before you could sell. In general, exercising an option is considered the equivalent of buying or selling the underlying instrument for margin and costing considerations.

Commissions are charged when an option is exercised. The commission charged will be the commission charged for executing an order on the underlying instrument for both the long and short of the option. For example, if you exercise a call option on American Widget stock, you will have to pay the commission to buy 100 shares of American Widget. This makes sense because when you exercise an option you are trading in the underlying instrument.

The true cost of exercise includes the transaction costs and the time premium, if any, remaining on the option. (Time premium is defined later in this chapter.) The costs make it expensive for most people to exercise options, so it is generally done only by exchange members.

You will not want to exercise an option unless it is bid at less than its intrinsic value. (We will discuss intrinsic value later in this chapter.) This will occur only if the option is very deep in-the-money (in-the-money will be discussed later in this chapter) or very near expiration. An option can be abandoned if the premium left is less than the transaction costs of liquidating it.

Options that are in-the-money are almost certain to be exercised at expiration. The only exceptions are those options that are less in-the-money than the transaction costs to exercise them at expiration.

For example, a soybean option that is only .25 cent in-the-money (worth $12.50) will not be exercised by most investors because the transaction costs will be greater than the $12.50 received by exercising. In all other cases, in the-money options should be exercised. Otherwise, you will lose the premium and gain nothing. Most option exercises occur within a few days of expiration because the time premium has dropped to a negligible or nonexistent level.

Most exchanges have automatic exercise of options that are in-the-money by a certain amount.

Prior to expiration, any option trading for less than the intrinsic value could also be exercised. This premature exercise can also occur if the price is far enough below the carrying costs relative to the underlying instrument. This discount is extremely rare, because arbitrageurs keep values in line. Even if it occurred, it is likely that only exchange members could capitalize on it because of their lower transaction costs.

A discount may occur when the underlying instrument is about to pay a dividend or interest payment. Following the payment, the price of the instrument will typically drop the equivalent of the dividend or interest payment. The option may have enough sellers before the dividend or interest payment to create the discount. There are typically a large number of sellers just before a dividend or interest payment because holders of calls do not receive the dividend or interest and therefore do not want to hold the option through the period when the payment causes the option price to dip.

In the final analysis, there are few exercises before the final few days of trading because it is not economically rational to exercise if there is any time premium remaining on the option.

HOW TO DESCRIBE AN OPTION

Exchange-traded options are standardized instruments. Each element contained in an option is set by the exchanges. The only element open to negotiation between buyers and sellers is the price of the option. This standardization increases the liquidity of trading and makes possible the current huge volume in options.

It is easier to buy or sell an option when you only negotiate price rather than every detail in the contract. Options on real estate are examples where each detail must be negotiated; negotiation can take weeks or months before a deal is made. Exchange-traded option transactions, on the other hand, can be consummated in seconds.

It takes four specifications to describe an option:

1. What is the name of the underlying instrument?
2. What is the type of option: call or put?
3. What is the strike price?
4. When is expiration?

In addition, the price of the option can be in the description in many situations.

For example, an option described as the April PaineWebber 35 put at 3 3/8 describes a put option on PaineWebber stock with a strike of 35, a premium of 3 3/8, and expiration in April.

Let's look at each specification.

The Class or Underlying Instrument

An option is an option on *something*. A **class** of options is all the puts and calls on a particular underlying instrument. Thus, the logical first place to start when describing the option is to mention the underlying instrument. Some common descriptions of underlying instruments are:
S&P 100 Index
IBM
Treasury-bond futures

Most of us shorten the name of the underlying instrument to something more manageable than the S&P 100 index. Most people will shorten it to "S&P 100," or often to its ticker symbol: "OEX."

The Type (Call or Put)

Is the option a put or a call? A call gives you the right but not the obligation to buy something and a put gives you the right but not the obligation to sell something.

The Strike Price

The third element is the strike price, also called the exercise price or striking price. A call gives the right to buy an underlying instrument while a put gives the right to sell an underlying instrument at a set price. The set price for these transactions is the strike price. For example, if you bought an OEX 250 call, you would have the right to buy the cash equivalent of the OEX index at 250 at any time during the life of the option. For another example, if you bought a gold 400 put, you would have the right to sell gold at $400 an ounce at any time during the life of the option. The strike price is, in effect, the predetermined price that the buyer and seller of an option have agreed upon.

Each option on an underlying instrument will have multiple strike prices. For example, the OEX option may have strike prices for puts and calls of 170, 175, 180, 185, 190, 195, 200, and 205. In general, the current price of the underlying instrument will be near the middle of the range of the strike prices.

The table, opposite, shows the usual interval between strike prices for some options currently traded.

In general, the higher the price of the underlying instrument, the wider the strike price. For example, Apple Computer, selling for less than $25 per share, has strike prices 2.50 apart. Teledyne, selling for greater than $200, has 10 between each strike price.

Option	Distance	Strike Price Example
Stock indexes		
S&P 100	5.00	195.00/200.00
Major Market Index	5.00	255.00/260.00
NYSE Composite	5.00	115.00/120.00
Value Line	5.00	205.00/210.00
Stocks		
IBM	5.00	135.00/140.00
General Motors	5.00	60.00/65.00
Apple Computer	2.50	17.50/20.00
Teledyne	10.00	280.00/290.00
Futures options		
Treasury-Bonds	2.00	90.00/92.00
Gold	20.00	320.00/340.00
Deutschemarks	1.00	33.00/34.00
S&P 500	5.00	195.00/200.00
Cash currencies		
British Pound	5.00	140-00/145-00
Canadian Dollar	1.00	72.00/73.00
Japanese Yen	1.00	195.00/200.00
Cash bonds		
10 5/8% of 2015	2.00	104-00/106-00

The exchanges add strike prices as the price of the UI changes. For example, let's say March Treasury-bond futures are listed at 80-00.

The Chicago Board of Trade (CBOT), the exchange where bond futures options are traded, may begin trading with strike prices ranging from 76-00 to 84-00. If bond futures trade up to 82-00, the exchange may add a 86-00 strike price. The more volatile the underlying instrument, the more strike prices there tend to be.

The Expiration Day

Options have finite lives. The expiration day of the option is the last day that the option owner can exercise the option.

This distinction is necessary to differentiate between American and European options. American options can be exercised any time before the expiration date at the owner's discretion. Thus, the expiration and exercise days can be different. European options can only be exercised on the expiration day. If exercised, the exercise and expiration days are the same. Unless otherwise noted, this book will discuss only American options.

Expiration dates are in regular cycles, and are determined by the exchanges. For example, a common stock expiration cycle is January/April/July/October. This means that options will be traded that expire in those months. Thus, a May IBM 125 call will expire in May if no previous action is taken by the holder. The exchanges add new options as old ones expire. The Chicago Board Options Exchange (CBOE) will list a July 1988 series of options when the October 1987 series expires. The exchanges limit the number of expiration dates usually to the nearest three. For example, stock options are only allowed to be issued for a maximum of nine months. Thus, only three expiration series will exist at a single time. Because of this, the option closest to expiration will be called the near- or short-term option, the second option to expire will be the medium- or middle-term option, and the third option will be called the far- or long-term option.

The following table shows the expiration cycles for some of the major types of options. Note that typically only the three nearest options will be trading at any time.

Option	Cycle
Stock indexes months	Monthly, using nearest three to four
Stocks	January/April/July/October February/May/August/November March/June/September/December Monthly, using nearest three months
Futures options	Corresponding to the delivery cycle of underlying futures contract
Spot currencies	March/June/September/December but monthly for nearest three months
Cash bonds	March/June/September/December

The Premium

The price of an option is called the premium. The buyer of an option pays the premium to the seller. The premium is negotiated and set when the option is bought or sold. The negotiation is in the form of an open outcry auction on the floor of the various exchanges.

In-the-money, Out-of-the-money, and At-the-money

Other terms to describe options are *in-the-money, out-of-the-money,* and *at-the-money.* This describes the relationship between option prices and the price of the underlying instrument. A call option is in-the-money if the price of the underlying instrument is higher than the strike price. A put option is in-the-money if the price of the underlying instrument is lower than the strike price. A call option is out-of-the-money if the price of the underlying instrument is below the strike price. A put option is out-of-the-money if the price of the underlying instrument is above the strike price. In tabular form:

Option	Relationship	Description
Call	UI higher than strike	In-the-money
Call	UI lower than strike	Out-of-the-money
Put	UI higher than strike	Out-of-the-money
Put	UI lower than strike	In-the-money

An at-the-money option is one in which the price of the underlying instrument is equivalent to the strike price. Most people use at-the-money to also describe the strike price that is closest to the price of the underlying instrument.

Changes in Option Specifications

The terms of an option contract can change after being listed and traded. This is very infrequent and happens only in stock options when the stock splits or pays a stock dividend. The result is a change in the strike prices and the number of shares that are deliverable.

A stock split will increase the number of options contracts outstanding and reduce the strike price. For example, suppose that Exxon declares a two for one split. You will be credited with having twice as many contracts, but the strike price will be halved. If you owned 20 Exxon 45 calls before the split, you will have 40 Exxon 22 1/2 calls following the split. Note that the new strike prices can be fractional.

A stock dividend has the same effect on the number of options and the strike price. For example, Merrill Lynch declares a 5 percent stock dividend. The exchange will adjust the number of shares in a contract up to 105 from 100 and reduce the strike price by 5 percent. An old call with a strike price of 50 will now be listed as the 47 1/2 call.

Exchanges will list new strikes at round numbers following the split or stock dividend. The fractional strikes disappear as time passes.

THE OPTION CHART

The option chart is a key diagram that will show up throughout the book. It shows the profit or loss of an option strategy at various prices of the underlying instrument at expiration. Figure 2.1 shows an options chart. The scale on the left shows the profit or loss of the option. The bottom scale shows the price of the underlying instrument.

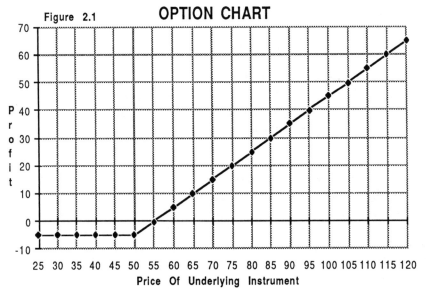

Figure 2.1 — OPTION CHART

The chart illustrates the key fact that the price of an option generally rises and falls when the price of the underlying instrument rises and falls. Thus, a call option buyer is bullish and the seller is bearish. A put option buyer is bearish and the seller is bullish. For example, if the price of Widget International was $30 and you were holding a July Widget 40 put, you could exercise the option and make $10 per share. If the stock dropped to $25, you would make $15 by exercising. By exercising the put, you have taken stock you can buy for $25 in the open market and *put* it to someone else for the strike price of $40. Your purchase price is $25, your sale price is $40, and your profit is therefore $15.

PRICE QUOTES

Price quotes are essentially like the quotes of the underlying instrument. Figure 2.2, opposite, shows a typical option price table from a newspaper. The rows are for the prices of the various strike prices while the columns are for calls and puts and the various expirations. With few exceptions, the units of price are the same as the underlying instrument. For example, a price of 4 3/8 for an option on a stock means a cost of $437.50 for the option. Each option is for 100 shares, and therefore the price for the option is 100 times the cost-per-share of the option, 4 3/8

Quotations for options on Treasury-bond and Treasury-note futures are quoted in 64s, while the underlying futures are quoted in 32s. Many people make trading mistakes when trading these options due to this difference.

Price quotes on quotation services will be priced the same, but each quotation service has a different code for each option. Consult with your quotation service for the quote symbol of the option you are interested in.

Options quotes are available on the previous day's close in the *Wall Street Journal, Investor's Daily*, and almost all big-city dailies. Quotes are available on all the major quotations services, such as Quotron and Bunker-Ramo. They are also available on telephone computer services, such as Dow-Jones News Retrieval and Compuserve. You can also call your broker for quotes.

COMMISSIONS

Options commissions are calculated differently at each brokerage house. There are, however, two main styles of calculation.

Chicago Board Options Exchange

Option & NY Close	Strike Price	Calls-Last Feb	Calls-Last Mar	Calls-Last Apr	Puts-Last Feb	Puts-Last Mar	Puts-Last Apr
AGreet	25	r	r	2 3/8	r	s	r
27 1/8	30	1/16	3/16	3/4	r	r	r
Amrtch	130	r	r	r	r	r	1
141 1/4	135	6 1/4	r	r	7/8	r	r
141 1/4	140	3	r	r	2 1/2	r	4 1/4
141 1/4	145	1 1/8	r	2 7/8	r	r	r
Atl R	55	r	s	13	r	s	r
68 3/4	60	r	s	8 1/2	r	s	1/2
68 3/4	65	3 3/4	r	4 7/8	1/2	1 3/8	1 5/8
68 3/4	70	7/8	r	2	r	r	4 1/2
BankAm	10	s	s	r	s	s	1/16
15 1/8	12 1/2	2 3/4	r	2 3/4	r	r	r
15 1/8	15	9/16	7/8	1 1/16	7/16	5/8	15/16
15 1/8	17 1/2	1/8	1/4	5/16	r	r	2 1/2
BellAtl	70	3 3/8	r	4 1/4	r	r	r
73 1/8	75	3/4	1 1/4	1 1/2	r	3	r
73 1/8	80	s	s	1/4	s	s	r
Chryslr	30	s	17	s	s	r	s
47 7/8	35	r	13	12	r	1/16	1/8
47 7/8	40	8	8 1/4	8 3/8	1/16	1/4	7/16
47 7/8	45	3 3/4	4 1/4	4 5/8	11/16	1 1/4	1 5/8
47 7/8	50	1 3/16	2	2 5/8	3 7/8	4	4 3/4
Citicp	45	s	s	r	s	s	1/16
58 3/8	50	r	r	8 5/8	1/16	r	r
58 3/8	55	3 1/2	3 5/8	4 3/4	1/2	r	1 1/4
58 3/8	60	7/8	1 3/8	1 15/16	2 3/4	r	r
Cullin	7 1/2	r	r	1 1/4	1/4	r	r
8 1/8	10	1/8	r	1/2	r	r	2 1/8
Delta	45	r	s	11 1/4	1/16	s	r
56 1/2	50	6 3/8	r	7 3/8	3/16	3/8	1/2
56 1/2	55	2 1/2	2 3/4	3 5/8	1	1 3/8	2 1/4
56 1/2	60	5/8	1 1/8	1 5/8	r	r	6
EKodak	55	s	s	22	s	s	1/8
77 3/4	60	s	s	16 3/4	s	s	r
77 3/4	65	r	s	13	r	s	5/16
77 3/4	70	7 3/4	7 3/4	9	1/4	5/8	15/16
77 3/4	75	3 3/8	5	5 1/4	1	r	2 1/4
77 3/4	80	1 1/4	1 7/8	2 3/8	3 1/4	r	r
Exxon	65	r	s	r	r	s	1/4
80	70	7 7/8	r	9 7/8	1/8	r	5/16
80	75	5	r	5 3/4	3/8	7/8	1 1/8
80	80	1 7/16	2 1/4	2 7/8	2 1/2	3	3
80	85	1/4	r	1	r	r	r
FedExp	55	s	s	r	s	s	15/16
64 1/8	60	r	r	r	5/8	1 1/4	2
64 1/8	65	2 1/8	2 9/16	3 3/4	r	3 1/2	3 3/4
64 1/8	70	5/8	r	1 1/2	r	r	r
64 1/8	75	s	s	5/8	s	s	r
Grumm	25	2 1/8	r	r	r	r	r
26 5/8	30	1/16	r	9/16	r	r	r
Halbtn	25	4 7/8	5	r	1/16	r	r
29 3/4	30	3/4	1 1/8	1 1/2	r	r	1 7/8
29 3/4	35	r	r	7/16	r	r	r
HomeSh	15	s	s	r	s	s	1/8
38 1/2	17 1/2	r	s	24	1/8	s	3/8
38 1/2	20	18 1/2	s	18	1/4	s	3/8
38 1/2	22 1/2	15 1/4	s	16 3/4	3/16	s	11/16
38 1/2	25	12 1/2	r	14	5/8	1 3/8	1 1/2
38 1/2	27 1/2	12 1/4	s	12 1/2	1 1/8	s	2 1/2
38 1/2	30	9	10 1/2	10 1/8	1 5/8	3 1/4	3 3/8
38 1/2	35	6 1/4	7 1/2	8 5/8	3 1/2	5 1/2	5 3/4
38 1/2	40	4 1/8	5 1/4	6 1/8	5 1/2	7	8 1/2
38 1/2	45	2 1/2	3 1/2	4 1/2	r	r	r
Homstk	22 1/2	r	s	r	1/16	s	r
27 5/8	25	r	r	3 3/4	3/8	5/8	3/4
27 5/8	30	3/8	5/8	15/16	r	r	3 1/8
27 5/8	35	s	s	1/4	s	s	r
B M	110	r	14 1/2	16 1/4	1/8	3/8	5/8
127 1/8	115	12	11 1/4	14 1/4	5/16	13/16	1 1/8
127 1/8	120	8 1/8	8 7/8	10 1/8	1	1 7/8	2 1/4
127 1/8	125	4 3/8	5 5/8	6 3/4	2 1/2	3 1/2	4 3/8
127 1/8	130	2 1/8	3 1/4	4 3/8	5 3/8	6 1/8	7
127 1/8	135	s	s	2 3/4	s	s	10 1/2
127 1/8	140	s	s	1 9/16	s	s	r
127 1/8	145	s	s	9/16	s	s	r
127 1/8	150	s	s	1/2	s	s	r
In Pap	75	r	s	16 1/2	r	s	5/8
90 7/8	80	9 1/4	r	11	1/8	r	7/8
90 7/8	85	6 1/2	s	8	1	s	2 1/2
90 7/8	90	3 1/2	5	5 1/4	3	3 7/8	4 1/2
90 7/8	95	1 1/4	2 1/4	3	r	r	r
90 7/8	100	r	r	1 3/4	r	r	r

The first and simplest method is the flat rate. Here, the broker makes a single charge for each option. For example, a broker could charge $100 for executing a gold option trade.

Another common method is to charge a percentage of the value of the premium. For example, your broker could charge you 5 percent of the premium. You would be charged $100 if you bought a stock option for $20. The value of the option is $2000 (100 shares times $20), and 5 percent of the premium is $100.

Some brokers will combine the two styles. For example, you could be charged 5 percent of the premium, but with a minimum of $30 and a maximum of $100.

It is important to keep commission costs to a minimum no matter what strategy your broker uses. A reduction in trading costs can have a big impact on your bottom line at the end of the year. The increase in return in percentage terms is particularly important for hedged options strategies, like covered writes, because they have two or more commissions for each trade.

However, the cheapest commissions may be a false economy. Be sure to look at the total package from the brokerage house. You may pay fewer commissions but not receive any support or perhaps poor order execution. The cheapest brokerage house could turn out to be the most expensive!

ORDERS

Option orders are the same as orders for stock indexes, stocks, or futures. In general, the accepted orders for options are the same as those accepted for the underlying instrument. We will mention special considerations about orders when necessary in the rest of the book.

DETERMINANTS OF OPTIONS PRICES

In the final analysis, option prices are set by the negotiations of buyers and sellers. Prices of options are influenced mainly by the expectations of future prices of the buyers and sellers and the relationship of the option's price with the price of the UI. Let us first take a look at the components of the price and then outline the factors that effect the option price.

The Components of the Price

An option's price or premium has two components: intrinsic value and extrinsic value. The intrinsic value of an option is a function of its price and the strike price. The intrinsic value equals the in-the-money amount of the options. For example, a United Widget 160 call will have an intrinsic value of 15 if the underlying instrument is 175. The intrinsic value of an at- or out-of-the-money option is zero. Thus, an out-of-the-money option is an option with only extrinsic value.

The extrinsic value is usually referred to as the time value. The time value is the amount that the price of the option exceeds the intrinsic value. Time value reflects the amount of risk of the option attaining in-the-money status. Its value is found using the simple formula:

Time value = option premium - intrinsic value

Alternately, the time value for in-the-money calls and puts is:

Call time value = option price + strike price - price of UI

Put time value = options price - strike price + price of UI

An option trading for its intrinsic value is trading at parity. Only in-the-money options can trade at parity. This usually occurs very close to expiration when the time value can easily be zero.

There are two ways to look at time value. The first is that time value is greatest on options with the greatest time until expiration. The second is that time value tends to be at its greatest when the UI is near the strike price for all those options that expire at the same time. Table 2.1 shows this phenomenon.

Table 2.1. Relationship of time value to strike price

Digital Equipment priced at 182 3/4

Strike price	May call price	Intrinsic value	Time value
165	19	17 3/4	1 1/4
170	15	12 3/4	2 1/4
175	11	7 3/4	3 1/4
180	7 7/8	2 1/4	5 5/8
185	4 7/8	0	4 7/8
190	3 1/8	0	3 1/8
195	2	0	2

The Factors that Influence Options Prices

Several key factors influence options prices. They are:
1. Price of the underlying instrument
2. Strike price
3. Time remaining until expiration
4. The risk-free rate
5. Expected volatility
6. Dividend or interest payments, if any

An option has a fair value. The fair value is the price the option should trade at given the five factors listed above. The concept of fair value has far-reaching implications. A common use of fair value is to calculate the expected price of an option given various combinations of these five factors. For example, you are thinking of buying an option but want to know what it will be priced at if the underlying instrument climbs $5, there are 10 less days to expiration, the expected volatility declines from 15 percent to 10 percent, and there is a dividend payment.

However, each person may use different assumptions and have different fair values. Calculations of this type are important for deciding if the price of the option is a good deal. You can compare your assumptions with those of the market to determine strategies.

Price of the Underlying Instrument

The price of the underlying instrument is the most important influence on an option price. In combination with the strike price, it determines if the option is in-the-money or out-of-the-money.

The delta or hedge ratio measures the relationship of changes in the prices of the option and the underlying instrument. The relationship between the option and the underlying instrument changes as the factors outlined here change, but the delta measures only the sensitivity of the option price to changes in the price of the underlying instrument. It is calculated using option evaluation formulas.

A delta of .50 means that the price of the option will move half as much as the price of the underlying instrument. For example, if the underlying instrument moves $5.00, the option will move $2.50.

The delta changes as the price of the underlying instrument changes. A deep in-the-money option will have a delta approaching 1.00, while a deep out-of-the-money will have a delta approaching 0.00. Figure 2.3 is an option value chart. This shows the price of the option at various prices of the underlying instrument and breaks the option price into intrinsic and time value (the shaded area). The delta is the slope of a line tangent to the price curve. As the price moves up the curve the slope increases, hence the delta increases. This also means that the delta changes with every change in price of the underlying instrument.

OPTION VALUE CHART

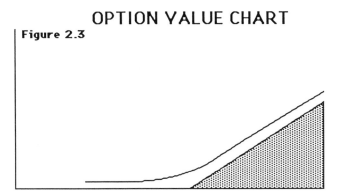

Figure 2.3

Price Of Underlying Instrument

Delta is usually referred to as a single number and, technically, this is correct. We can say that there are up and down deltas because the slope of the tangent line is changing in different directions as the price moves up or down the price curve. A delta of .50 suggests that the price of the option will move half as much as the price of the underlying instrument. However, if the price of the underlying moves higher, the delta will have increased and the price of the option will have moved more than half as much. For example, presume a delta of .50. If the price of the underlying increases $10, the option might actually increase by $6; the option might decrease by only $4 if the underlying drops $10.

The gamma is the amount that the delta moves with changes in the price of the underlying instrument. For example, if an option has a delta of .50 and a gamma of .05, then the delta will be .55 if the price of the underlying instrument rises one point, and .45 if the price falls one point. In effect, the gamma is the rate of change of the delta for each one-point move in the underlying instrument.

The delta is important for both traders and hedgers. Traders can use the delta to help identify the options with the most responsiveness to the underlying instrument. Hedgers need to know the delta to have the proper number of contracts to hedge their particular instrument.

Strike Price

The strike price has a major impact on the option price because it determines whether the option is in-the-money or out-of-the-money. Figure 2.4 is a call option value chart showing only the intrinsic value of an option. Note that there is no intrinsic value until the UI price is above the strike price.

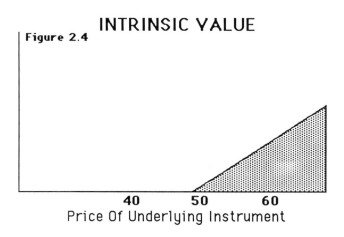

INTRINSIC VALUE

Figure 2.4

Price Of Underlying Instrument

Figure 2.5, on the following page, is an option value chart that shows the price of the option, including the intrinsic value and the time value (the shaded area). It shows that the time value is greatest when the UI price is at the strike price. This illustrates the same principle as Table 2.1. In addition, Figure 2.5 and Table 2.1 illustrate that the time value is lower as the price of the UI moves away from the strike price.

OPTION VALUE CHART

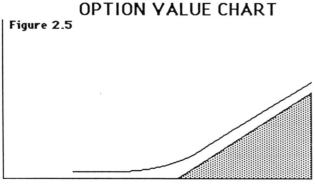

Figure 2.5

Price Of Underlying Instrument

This is important because it illustrates what happens to the option's price as the UI price changes. For example, let's say you bought a 65 call when the price was 50. As the price of the UI climbs, the option price climbs, but the components of the price change when the UI price surmounts the strike price. The components of the option price change from all time value to increasing intrinsic value. Notice also how the profits accelerate as prices approach and pass the strike price.

Time Remaining until Expiration

Figure 2.5 illustrates the situation some time prior to expiration. Options are called a wasting asset because their value declines over time. The time remaining until the exercise date increases in importance as the exercise date nears. When you buy an option you are paying for the right to buy or sell something. The option has a time limit. The value will naturally decline as time progresses, all other things being equal.

Figure 2.6, opposite, shows the option value curve at different times in the life of the option. This illustrates that the time value of the option declines as the expiration day approaches. In addition, it demonstrates that far options will always be priced higher than near options. The difference is greatest when the UI price is at the strike price, but declines as the UI price moves more in-the-money or out-of-the money.

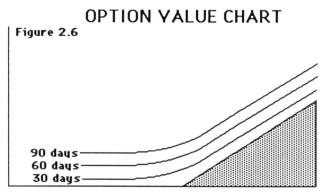

OPTION VALUE CHART

Figure 2.6

Price Of Underlying Instrument

Time value does not decline in a straight line. Instead, it declines very little in the early days of its life but declines more sharply the closer it is to expiration. Figure 2.7 shows the typical decline in value if everything else stays the same.

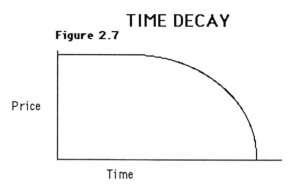

TIME DECAY

Figure 2.7

Price

Time

The time value decay accelerates as expiration nears. The rate of decay is roughly a function of the square root of the time remaining. You can estimate the relationship of the rate of decay of two different options by taking the square root of the months remaining on the longest option. For example, the rate of decay of a two-month option is twice that of a four-month option because the square root of four is two.

The rate of decay is called theta. This is the loss in theoretical value that will occur if another day passes, all other things being equal. For example, a theta of .005 means that the option will lose .5 of a price unit each day.

Interest Rates

The level of interest rates also affects the price of options. The higher interest rates are, the higher the premium will be for options. The reason is that options premiums are competing investments with debt instruments. Part of the pricing of an option premium is the so-called risk-free rate, which is usually considered to be the short-term Treasury-bill rate. Option pricing theory says that the return to an investor cannot be less than the risk-free rate for the same time period because the option is a much riskier investment and the returns must be higher.

Expected Volatility

The price of the option will be influenced by the expected and recent volatility of the underlying instrument. The more volatile an instrument is the more valuable the option will be. The reason is that increased volatility means there is a greater chance for the option to make money. For example, let's say you buy an out-of-the-money option with a strike of 60 and a price of 2 when the underlying instrument is 50. The price range of the instrument for the last year has been 48 to 52. Unless something dramatic occurs, it will be unlikely that the call will expire with any intrinsic value. On the other hand, a recent range of 25-75 suggests a much greater chance of success.

Investor's perceptions of future volatility are largely influenced by recent volatility. The option price is based on the expected volatility from the time of purchase to the time of expiration. Volatility may have been very low prior to initiating the position, but the market may expect the volatility to increase. Perhaps earnings estimates are due to be issued or there is a series of economic reports about to be released.

Volatility can play a large role in selecting option strategies because of its powerful effect. As an example, Table 2.2 shows the price of an at-the-money call with the price of the underlying instrument at 65 with 23 days remaining until expiration.

Table 2.2. Effect of volatility on option price

Volatility	Option price
10	.61
11	.67
12	.73
13	.79
14	.85
15	.91

The price of an option can be broken into various components. Models for determining the fair value of options can be turned on their head and used to compute the components of the current price. Implied volatility is often calculated because of its importance. The implied volatility of an option price is the expected volatility that is implied in the current option price.

The responsiveness of the option price to changes in the volatility is called vega. Vega measures how much the price of the option will change, given a 1 percent change in implied volatility. For example, a vega of .20 means that the price of the option will move .20 of a price unit for every percentage-point change in implied volatility.

One important concept for options trading is delta neutral. We will be referring to it often throughout the book. Delta neutral means that the net delta of the options position is neutral and has no market bias. For example, the delta of an underlying instrument is always 1.00 if you are long that instrument. An at-the-money option on that instrument will likely have a delta of .50. If you construct a covered write, for example, by buying the instrument and selling one call, your net delta is .50. Shorting the call changes the delta from positive to negative, so the net delta is computed by taking the delta of the instrument, 1.00, and subtracting the delta of the option, .50. This position could be changed to a delta neutral position by selling another call with a delta of .50. The total delta of the short option would be 1.00, exactly offsetting the 1.00 delta of the long instrument. Thus, this position would be delta neutral and have no market bias.

Dividend or Interest Payments, If Any

Dividends affect the price of an option particularly at the time that the payment is made. The value of the underlying instrument will rise each day, all other things being equal, until the day the dividend or interest is paid. This is because the value of the underlying instrument is increased by the impending payment. For example, a stock with a $1 dividend payment is worth more one day before the exdividend day than 30 days before. The reason is that the total return of buying the stock is greater one day before exdividend day because you will have that $1 dividend.

The day after the dividend payment is made, the price of the underlying instrument will drop approximately the same as the value of the payment. This affects the option as well. The option price will drop following the payment even though the option owner does not receive the payment. This also has the effect of reducing the value of options that pay high dividends relative to those that pay low or no dividends.

KEY OPTIONS CALCULATIONS

There are several key calculations necessary when trading options. What is the most amount of money I can make? What's the worst that could happen to me?

Size of Position

The size of the position can make a significant difference in your return. Commission costs and, to a lesser extent, financing costs are reduced per unit the more shares, stock index contracts, or futures contracts are written against. For example, a covered write program using GM stock will cost less per trade in commissions using 100,000 shares than using 100 shares. The net effect is that the greater the position, the higher your returns will be and the better your break-even point will be.

Importance of Price

The returns of any option strategy are affected by the price paid or received. This is particularly true with hedged strategies such as covered writes, spreads, combos, and straddles. The gain or loss of a tick can have a profound impact on the return of the investment. This means that you should be alert to not giving up that last eighth when entering a stock order.

Break-even Point

The break-even point is the price point where you neither make nor lose money on your investment. Each option strategy has a different break-even point. Figure 2.8, opposite, shows the break-even level for a purchase of a call. At 55, the gain in the price of the widget is equal to the cost of the call.

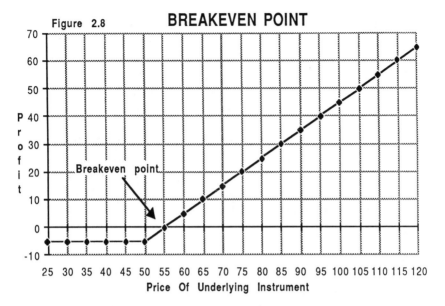

Figure 2.8   **BREAKEVEN POINT**

The break-even described here refers *only* to the break-even at the expiration of the option. You can lose money before the expiration of the contract if the price of the instrument declines. For example, suppose the instrument went to $45 on the first day after buying a call. The value of the call will have dropped below its $4.00 initial price, but not enough to offset the decline in value of the instrument. This is because the value of the call is composed mainly of time value rather than intrinsic value. The decline in the underlying instrument causes a decline in the price of the option but not to the same extent as if the option were in the money and had more intrinsic value. Don't forget: The simple break-even point describes the situation only at the expiration of the option.

Figure 2.6 shows the change in the break-even over time. Eventually, the position loses all its time value. The valuation curve illustrates the classic options curve.

The actual break-even point at expiration is the same as the simple point, but you must take into account transaction and carrying costs. Thus the formula is:

$$\text{Actual break-even point} = \text{Simple break-even point} - \text{transaction costs} + \text{carrying costs}$$

The break-even point is affected by many factors, primarily the type of account and transaction. For example, a trade using stocks can take place using cash or margin. The carrying cost for a cash transaction will only be the opportunity cost. The carrying cost for stock bought on margin includes the cost of financing for the additional stock.

Net Investment Required

The net investment required is the dollar amount necessary to initiate the trade. Each option strategy requires a different investment. A major determinant of the amount is the type of trade. Are you buying or writing the option? Is it a mixed transaction that involves options and other instruments? Is the trade going to use cash or will margin be used?

The Investment Return

It is just as important to know the return on your investment as it is to know your break-even point. There are several major ways to calculate the return on your investment. Each presents a different perspective on the proposed trade.

A key way to make comparisons between various strategies is to annualize the return. For example, you may expect to make 13 percent on one option strategy for 2 months but 9 percent on another strategy that you will hold for 1 month. You will likely prefer the 1-month investment because the annualized return of 108 percent (9 percent times 12 months equals 108 percent) is greater than the annualized yield of 78 percent of the other investment. However, you should use the annualized yields to compare two similar strategies, not to compare with other types of investments. For example, you make 9 percent for a one month investment, but you don't know what your return will be for the remaining 11 months of the year. You may be able to reinvest at only 5 percent and would have been better off investing in a certificate of deposit at 8 percent for a year.

Return if Exercised

The return if exercised should be examined if you are short an option. For example, in a covered call position, the return if exercised is the return on the investment if the underlying stock was called away. The return is also affected by the type of transaction and account.

Return if Unchanged

The return if unchanged is the return on your investment if there is no change in the price of the underlying instrument. This method of calculating return has a major advantage over the return if exercised; it makes no assumption about future prices.

Expected Return

The expected return is the possible return weighted by the probability of the outcome. The most common way to do this is to take the implied volatility and compute the probability of various prices based on the implied volatility. It is assumed that prices will describe a normal bell-shaped curve (though scientific studies suggest this is not accurate, it is usually close enough for virtually all option strategies). The precise math is beyond the scope of this book, but let us simply illustrate the principle.

Let's assume that the normal distribution of prices, as suggested by the implied volatility, implies that the chances are 66 percent that prices of XYZ Corp. will stay within a range of 50-60. Your position has been constructed to show a profit of $1000 if prices stay within that range. There is a 16.5 percent chance of prices trading above

$60 and a similar chance of prices trading below $50. You will lose $1000 if prices move above 60 or below 50. Your expected return is therefore the sum of the potential profits and losses times their respective chances of happening. Thus, the expected return would be (.66 times 1000) plus (.165 times -1000) plus (.165 times -1000) for a total of $330.

Return per Day

The return per day is the expected return per day until either expiration or the day you expect to liquidate the trade. For example, you may be comparing two covered call writing programs and want to know which one is best. Take the expected return and divide by the number of days until expiration. That way, you can compare two investments of differing lengths.

3

Selecting A Strategy

A. Strategy selection
B. Bullish strategies
C. Stable prices
D. Bearish strategies
E. Volatile prices
F. Time decay helps
G. Time decay mixed
H. Time decay hurts
I. Profit/loss characteristics

STRATEGY SELECTION

Selecting a strategy is a multistep process. Each step should lead to further refinement of the strategy. This chapter contains tables that show various simple attributes of the main strategies.

One problem with this type of effort is that it must, by necessity, simplify. For example, long straddles are considered neutral strategies but can actually be constructed with a market bias. The tables in this chapter refer to strategies as they are usually considered.

There are two major techniques to identifying an appropriate strategy.

First, identify your ideas on the major factors that affect options prices. You will need to look at such factors as market opinion, volatility, and time decay. You will then be able to make a statement like "I think that Widgets will move slightly higher in price, volatility will decline, and time premiums will decay rapidly because we are approaching expiration." You can then look through the tables to find the strategy that best fits your outlook. In this case, a covered call write position fits the bill.

The second method, which can easily be used in conjunction with the first, is to systematically rank various option strategies. For example, you may have decided that covered call writing fits your outlook. You now want to rank the covered calls on Widget International by their various risk/reward characteristics. For example, you could rank them by expected return, or perhaps the ratio of the return if unchanged to the down-side break-even point. The main problem with the use of rankings is that you'll probably need a computer to do all the possible mathematical manipulations.

The strategies in this book are generally presented in their plain vanilla form. Yet the very nature of options gives greater scope to the creative strategist.

For example, one of the interesting aspects of options is that you can combine strategies to create even more attractive opportunities. You could write a straddle and buy an underlying instrument to create a lower break-even than holding the underlying instrument alone, create greater profits if prices stagnate, but give up some of the up-side potential. You should be able to examine a myriad of fascinating strategies after reading this book.

Another feature of options is the ability to twist the expiration and strike prices to fit your outlook. For example, a straddle is constructed by buying a put and a call with the same strike price. That is the plain vanilla. But you can change the strike prices by, say, buying an out-of-the-money put and buying an out-of-the-money call and creating what is called a strangle. Or, why not buy the call for nearby expiration but the put for a far expiration? The net effect is that you have a tremendous tool in options for creating exciting trading opportunities. Do not get stuck in the ordinary.

BULLISH STRATEGIES

Buy call
Bull spread
Sell put
Covered call write
Buy instrument/buy put
Buy call/sell put

STABLE PRICES

Sell straddle
Sell strangle
Ratio write
Short butterfly
Ratio spreads

BEARISH STRATEGIES

Buy put
Bear spread
Sell call
Sell instrument/buy call
Covered put write
Buy put/sell call

VOLATILE PRICES

Buy straddle
Buy butterfly

TIME DECAY HELPS

Short call
Short put
Short straddle
Covered call write
Covered put write

TIME DECAY MIXED

Bull spread
Bear spread
Long butterfly
Short butterfly

TIME DECAY HURTS

Long call
Long put
Long straddle

PROFIT/LOSS CHARACTERISTICS

Strategy	Profit	Loss
Buy a call	Open	Limited
Buy a put	Open	Limited
Short a call	Limited	Open
Short a put	Limited	Open
Covered call write	Limited	Open
Covered put write	Limited	Open
Bull spread	Limited	Limited
Bear spread	Limited	Limited
Long butterfly	Limited	Limited
Short butterfly	Limited	Limited
Calendar spreads	Open	Open
Long straddle	Open	Limited
Short straddle	Limited	Open

4

Buy A Call

A. Strategy
B. Equivalent strategy
C. Risk/reward
D. Orders
E. Decision structure

STRATEGY

Buy a Call

Buying a call is a bullish strategy that requires a price rise in the underlying instrument. Nonetheless, the most critical factor in trading calls profitably is an ability to predict the future price moves of the underlying instrument. All the subsequent discussion on selecting a call in this chapter is secondary to the problem of market timing.

EQUIVALENT STRATEGY

Long Instrument/Long Put

The major difference between the long call and the long instrument/long put strategies is the commission. It will cost significantly less to simply buy a call.

However, many investors will buy a put to protect a profit or to provide a stop-loss point when they initiate a long instrument position. The net result is that they have duplicated a long call.

RISK/REWARD

Maximum Return

The maximum profit potential is theoretically unlimited. The profits climb as the price of the underlying instrument climbs. For example, a purchase of an OEX 220 call will gain one point for every point the underlying index gains if it is in-the-money at expiration. Before expiration, the call will move as the underlying instrument moves multiplied by the delta.

For example, assume a long OEX position at 149 and an April 150 call option with a premium of 4. Each point move of the OEX above the strike price of 150 will cause a move of at least one point in the call premium. Thus, the call premium on expiration would be 9850 if the OEX were at 10,000. Although the call profits are theoretically unlimited, as a practical matter, the profits will be proportional with the gains in the underlying instrument.

Break-even Point

The break-even point, at expiration, is the strike price plus the call premium. The simple break-even point for calls, in formula form:

Simple break-even point = strike price + call premium

The price of the underlying instrument must climb by some amount before expiration for you to make any money at expiration. For example, assume you have bought OEX 180 options at 12 and the OEX was at 175. If the option expires and the OEX is at 182, you will lose 10 points. The option gives you the right to buy the OEX at 180, which means the option has 2 points of intrinsic value with the OEX at 182. At expiration, the option has no time value. You therefore bought the option at 12 and, at expiration, it was worth 2. The OEX needed to rise to 192 before you would have profited.

You can lose money before the expiration of the contract if the price of the underlying instrument declines. For example, suppose the instrument went from 150 to 145 the first day after you bought a call. The value of the call will have dropped below its initial price. The amount of the drop is quantified by the delta of the call (see Chapter 2 - The Fundamentals of Options for details). The delta is largely dependent on whether the option is in- or out-of-the-money. An out-of-the-money call will usually not fall as much as an in-the-money call. This is because the value of an out-of-the-money call is time value rather than intrinsic value. The decline will be greater if the option is in-the-money because it will have more intrinsic value.

The actual break-even point is the same as the simple point, but includes transaction and carrying costs. Thus, the formula is:

Actual break-even point = simple break-even point - transaction costs + carrying costs

The break-even point is affected by the type of account and transaction. The trade can take place using cash or on margin. Transaction costs for margin trades will be more than for cash trades. The carrying cost for a cash transaction will only be the opportunity cost. Carrying costs for trades on margin include the financing for the additional quantity of the underlying instrument.

The Maximum Risk

The maximum risk is the premium paid for the option. For example, your risk on the purchase of an Exxon call at 4 3/8 is $437.50. You cannot lose more than the initial premium cost plus transaction and carrying costs.

Net Investment Required

Purchasing calls is always a debit transaction; you must pay the premium. For example, you must pay $1500 to buy a call on Treasury-bond futures if the price is 1 1/2. Another example is that you will pay $750 for 10 stock options with a premium of .75 each.

The Investment Return

The investment return on a call is the profit or loss divided by the initial investment. The formula is:

Return = (profit or loss) / initial investment

For example, if you buy an IBM option for 5 and sell it for 7 1/2, for a profit of 2 1/2, your return on investment is 50 percent (2 1/2 divided by 5 equals .50 or 50 percent). Annualizing the return will give you another perspective on the return. If this particular trade covered three months from beginning to end, you would have made a 200 percent annualized return.

However, in most cases, the return on investment is not the major criterion in buying a call. The main reason for buying a call is leverage. You can gain large percentage gains with a small investment. The low price of calls makes discussions of rates of return almost meaningless when examined on a trade-by-trade basis. Many of your trades may make 200 percent, but your losses may be 100 percent. These are large percentages simply because the initial investment is so low.

ORDERS

You can use just about any type of order for entering and exiting long calls. However, it is recommended that you use some type of limit order when trading options with little liquidity. (See Chapter 2 - The Fundamentals Of Options for more information on the types of orders.)

DECISION STRUCTURE

Selecting a Call

Selecting which call to buy requires an examination of expiration date, strike price, and price.

Expiration Date

The selection of the expiration date is largely dependent on when you expect the price of the underlying instrument to rally. If you believe that the up-move in price is imminent, buy the nearby expiration. It will respond the most to the up-move and provide the greatest leverage because it will have a higher delta than farther expirations. In addition, its time value will be less than that of farther expiration months and will therefore be less expensive, while providing greater profits. Consider buying the farther expiration months if you are unsure when the market will make its move or if you think the market may be steady, but you want to make sure you don't miss the move. The relative prices are also important. You may want to pay a higher price for a farther month just to have more time for the trade to work. The extra time premium may be a cheap price to pay for several more months for the trade to work. However, most traders do not hold positions very long, and the extra price may be a waste of time.

Strike Price

Your market attitude determines which strike price to select. The more bullish you are, the higher the strike you should select. Calls with higher strike prices require a larger up-side move before they are profitable on the last day of trading. Calls with lower strike prices require smaller moves to the up-side before they are profitable at expiration. Once the high strike call goes into the money, its percentage return skyrockets. The main reason is that the investment is so much lower than for lower strike prices. Nonetheless, the rule is that higher strike calls have a greater percentage return than lower strike calls *if they go sufficiently in the money.*

If you are very bullish on the underlying instrument, then buy out-of-the-money calls. The highest strike price is the most bullish. This will give you the greatest profit potential on a percentage basis, though there is less chance of success because the market has to rally farther before the call is in the money. If you are less bullish and want a greater chance of success, buy in-the-money calls. The lowest strike price is the least bullish choice. You will be cutting your potential percentage return but will have a greater chance of success, because the intrinsic value of the in-the-money calls gives you an advantage.

In effect, the out-of-the-money call has fewer dollars to risk but a greater probability of loss. For example, the price of the underlying instrument could rise slightly. You could lose money by having an out-of-the-money option, but still make money with an in-the-money option. In addition, the chances of an in-the-money option expiring worthless are less than for an out-of-the-money option.

You will be better off buying an in-the-money option if you are looking for a quick move, because the higher delta will respond immediately to any price change in the underlying instrument. Out-of-the-money options will require a greater move in the underlying instrument to get the same dollar gain. The choice then becomes which of the two types will give the greatest percentage return on the investment given your price expectation.

The net effect is that an out-of-the-money call will give you greater returns on large price moves of the underlying instrument, but the in-the-money call will provide superior returns if the underlying instrument only rises moderately.

Many investors buy out-of-the-money calls because they are less expensive. This is a poor reason to buy a call. If you have so few funds that you cannot afford in-the-money calls, then you are probably speculating needlessly and taking on too much risk.

Price

The price you pay for the call is the final consideration for selecting a call. Examining the factors that influence the price will determine if you are getting a good price, and give further clues to how the price of your selected options will behave. The major factor to consider is the expected volatility. Occasionally, consider expected changes in interest rates and, in some cases, expected dividend payments. The point of examining the factors that influence prices is to discover options that are undervalued relative to your estimate of the fair value of the option.

Expected Volatility

The expected volatility is the most important factor affecting your estimate of the fair value, and has a major impact on the selection of an option. If the volatility is expected to increase, the price of the option will be expected to increase, all other things being equal. You will need to have an option evaluation service or computer program to calculate the effect of an increase or decrease in volatility on the position.

A decrease in volatility will have an adverse effect on your position. You must carefully weigh the effects of a decline in volatility versus your expected price move in the underlying instrument. Once again, a computer program or service that details implied volatilities and the effect of changes in implied volatility on the option is extremely important. It is quite possible to get an expected move in the underlying instrument, but then to lose money on the call because the volatility declined.

A ramification of this is that you should select calls on the basis of the expected volatility versus their current price. For example, assume that two underlying instruments are trading for the same price, but the first one has a volatility three times that of the second one. That means that the options on the first instrument will be priced significantly higher than those of the second instrument. If the options on the first instrument are priced below a level that compensates for the greater volatility, it represents a better deal than the second option.

Systematic Call Selection

Most people view the selection of which call to buy as entirely derived from their projections of the price of the underlying instrument. This is certainly a valid procedure. But you can also examine the risk/reward of various calls first without looking at the merits of the underlying instrument. One method is to list calls in various rankings. For example, you could list all calls by their risk/reward characteristics given certain market moves. Note that you could examine all flavors of options, from OEX to soybeans, and apply the same criteria. Or you could focus on just those options in a group that you have selected through other means.

Suppose you think computer-industry stocks will go up in price but you don't know which stock or option to buy because you don't pick specific stocks. You could rank the options of the computer stocks by criteria that fit your trading style.

As a suggestion, consider ranking the options by a risk/reward ratio. First, pick a time horizon. For example, you expect the move to higher prices to occur over the coming three months. Assume that each stock in the industry group will move either up or down by the amount of the implied volatility. Alternately, assume that they will move higher or lower by your expected volatility. Note that we are assuming that the price could move both up and down, even though we are examining these particular stocks because we think they will rally. We do this so we may estimate their prices after both rises and falls so that we may estimate the reward from the expected rally and the risk if we are wrong.

Thus, we take the implied or estimated volatility for each stock, and estimate the price of the options given a price movement equal to the volatility during the time period, and then divide the resulting bullish option price by the bearish option price. The resulting ratio will give an excellent guide to the relative risk and reward of holding various options.

If the Price of the Underlying Instrument Drops

There are four possible strategies. First, if you are now bearish, liquidate the trade. The other three strategies are for use only if you are still bullish.

The first strategy is to hold your current position. This is often the best choice if there is little premium left and therefore little dollar risk in holding the position. However, it is not a good strategy if there is little time left on the option and the market would have to rally substantially to hit your break-even point.

The second choice is rolling down. This strategy entails selling two of your current calls and buying a call with a lower strike price. Your position will then be long one call with a lower strike price and short one call with your original strike price. In effect, you have rolled out of your long call position into a bull call spread (see Chapter 12 - Bull Spreads for more details). One critical factor is to try to buy the lower strike price for about the same price as the combined prices of the two calls you sold. For example, try to buy the OEX 140 calls at 5 if you can sell the two OEX 150 calls for 2 1/2 each.

This strategy does not require the sharp rally in the underlying instrument to make money. It therefore puts you in a better position to gain. The sacrifice is that the profit potential is reduced significantly. The net result is that the break-even point is lowered, the dollar risk stays about the same, but the maximum profit potential is also reduced. Another way to look at it is that the chance of success has been improved but the return from that success has been reduced.

Another strategy for holders of intermediate- or long-term calls is to sell a near-term call. For example, you are holding the July OEX 150 calls and the price of the underlying index declines. You could sell an April OEX 150 call, creating a calendar spread (see Chapter 15 - Calendar Spreads for more details). Basically, you are trying to capture the time premium on the near call as a method of lowering the cost of the far call. This strategy is particularly attractive if the near call is about to expire and the time premium is decaying rapidly. Then, if the underlying instrument rallies, you will still have the original call but at a lower price.

Investors must be very cautious when using this strategy, however, because they have initiated a bearish position. A sharp rally in the underlying instrument while you are holding the short near call will probably create more losses in the near call than profits in the far call. Thus, you should be very sure that the market will not zoom higher over the near term.

If the Price of the Underlying Instrument Rises

If you are now bearish, liquidate the trade and take your profits.

You have several choices if you are still bullish:

1. Sell a higher strike and hold your existing call.
2. Sell your existing position and buy a higher strike.
3. Hold your existing call.

The first choice turns your long call into a bull call spread. This strategy costs nothing except the extra commission, though you may need to post additional margin, depending on the option. You will need a margin account if you are going to do this with stock options. You have essentially locked in your profit, but you have still retained more profit opportunity. This strategy will be best if the market only climbs a little more or is stable. The bull call strategy will have the worst performance if the market continues to rally strongly. It's not that you will lose money, but the profits will not be as high as with the two other strategies. The profit potential, though, is reduced to the difference between the strike prices. For example, you bought an OEX 150 call and the price of the underlying index has rallied. You could sell the OEX 170 call, lock in your profit, and retain the possibility of a further profit of 20 points, the difference between the two strike prices. (See Chapter 12 - Bull Spreads for more details on the ramifications of this strategy.)

The most aggressive approach, called rolling up, is to liquidate your current position and buy another call but at a higher strike price. This is the best strategy if you are very bullish. Note, though, that the market must rise to above the new break-even point for you to make money on the new position. Thus, a stable or even slightly higher market will cause this strategy to be the worst of the three. For example, assume you bought an OEX 150 call at 5, it currently trades at 15, and the OEX 170 calls are trading for 3. You could liquidate the OEX 150s, take the 10-point profit, and invest 3 in the OEX 170 calls. Notice that you have taken out the money you initially invested and are now using only your profits to invest with.

The third strategy is to hold to your existing strategy. This is best if you are looking for a moderate move higher, but is the worst if the market drops below the original break-even point. Note that this is the riskiest of the three strategies because it is the only one that could have a loss on the whole series of transactions. For example, you bought the OEX 150 calls at 5 and they have gone to 15. The other two strategies lock in some of the profit at this point. Holding the existing position will lose money if the price of the OEX drops below the break-even point.

Further changes in the risk/reward situation can be accomplished by changing the number of contracts used in each strategy. For example, you could sell twice as many calls as you have long calls in the bull call strategy. This is obviously a more bearish strategy than writing the same number of calls as you originally bought. The price of the underlying could now probably drop, and you would still make a profit. Or how about buying twice as many calls when you roll up? You are now taking a much more bullish stance in the market.

If the Option is About to Expire

Another consideration is the time left on the position. Time decay accelerates near option expiration, which makes holding options less attractive. Your choices are the same as initiating a new trade. The additional wrinkle is that time decay is a more important consideration near expiration. In general, if you are still bullish, you should roll forward into the next expiration month as a tactic to reduce the impact of the time decay. If you are now bearish, liquidate the trade before all the time premium decays.

Another decision is whether or not to exercise. You will never want to exercise if the option has any time premium. This is because the exercise of the option will cause you to lose the remaining time premium.

In general, it is unwise to exercise if there is a cost to the exercise process. For example, it costs extra commissions to exercise a stock option because commissions must be paid on the purchase of the stock. On the other hand, there is automatic exercise of many futures options where the cost is neglible. In most cases, you are better off buying back the call if the premium is greater than the cost of commissions.

5

Buy A Put

A. Strategy
B. Equivalent Strategy
C. Risk/reward
D. Orders
E. Decision structure

STRATEGY

Buy a Put

Buying a put is a bearish strategy that requires a price drop in the underlying instrument. Nonetheless, the most critical factor in trading puts profitably is an ability to predict the future price moves of the underlying instrument. All the subsequent discussion on selecting a put in this chapter is secondary to the problem of market timing.

EQUIVALENT STRATEGY

Short Instrument/Long Call

The major difference in the long-put and the short-instrument/long-call strategies is the commission. It is significantly less expensive to simply buy a put.

However, some investors will buy a call to protect a profit or to provide a stop-loss point when they initiate a short sale of the instrument. The net result is that they have duplicated a long put.

RISK/REWARD

Maximum Return

The maximum profit potential is limited by the fact that the price of the underlying instrument cannot go below zero. The profits climb as the price of the underlying instrument drops. For example, a purchase of an OEX 220 put will gain one point for every point the underlying index drops if it is in-the-money at expiration. Before expiration, the price change of the put will be equal to the price change of the underlying instrument multiplied by the delta.

For example, assume the OEX is trading at 151 and the April 150 put option has a premium of $4. Each point move of the OEX below the strike price of 150 will cause a move of 1 point in the put premium. Thus, the put premium on expiration would be 149 if the OEX were at 1. Although the put profits are theoretically limited, as a practical matter, the profits will be proportional with the price drops of the underlying instrument.

Break-even Point

The break-even point, at expiration, is the strike price minus the put premium. The simple break-even point for puts, in formula form:

Simple break-even point = strike price - put premium

The price of the underlying must drop by some amount before expiration for you to make any money at expiration. For example, assume you have bought OEX 180 options at 12 and the OEX was at 185. If the option expires and the OEX is at 178, you will lose 10 points. The option gives you the right to sell the OEX at 180, which means the option has 2 points of intrinsic value with the OEX at 178. At expiration, the option has no time value. You therefore bought the option at 12 and, at expiration, it was worth 2. The OEX needed to fall to 168 before you would have profited.

You can lose money before the expiration of the contract if the price of the underlying instrument climbs. For example, suppose the instrument went from 150 to 155 the first day after you bought a put. The value of the put will have dropped below its initial price. The amount of the drop is quantified by the delta of the call (see Chapter 2 - The Fundamentals Of Options for details). The delta is largely dependent on whether the option is in- or out-of-the-money. An out-of-the-money put will usually not fall as much as an in-the-money put. This is because the value of an out-of-the-money put is time value rather than intrinsic value. The decline will be greater if the option is in-the-money because it will have more intrinsic value.

The actual break-even point is the same as the simple point, but includes transaction and carrying costs. Thus, the formula is:

Actual break-even point = simple break-even point - transaction costs + carrying costs

The break-even point is affected by the type of account and transaction. The trade can take place using cash or on margin. Transaction costs for margin trades will be more than for cash trades. The carrying cost for a cash transaction will only be the opportunity cost. Carrying costs for trades on margin include the financing for the additional quantity of the underlying instrument.

The Maximum Risk

The maximum risk is the premium paid for the option. For example, your risk on the purchase of an Exxon call at 4 3/8 is $437.50. You cannot lose more than the initial premium cost plus transaction and carrying costs.

Net Investment Required

Purchasing puts is always a debit transaction; you must pay the premium. For example, you must pay $1500 to buy a put on Treasury-bond futures if the price is 1 1/2. You will pay $750 for 10 stock options with a premium of .75 each.

The Investment Return

The investment return on a put is the profit or loss divided by the initial investment. The formula is:

Return = (profit or loss) / initial investment

For example, if you buy an IBM option for 5 and sell it for 7 1/2, for a profit of 2 1/2, your return on investment is 50 percent (2 1/2 divided by 5 equals .50, or 50 percent). Annualizing the return will give you another perspective on the return. If this particular trade covered 3 months from beginning to end, you would have made a 200 percent annualized return.

However, in most cases, the return on investment is not the major criterion of buying a put. The main reason for buying a put is leverage. You can gain large percentage gains with a small investment. The low price of puts make discussions of rates of return almost meaningless when examined on a trade by trade basis. Many of your trades may make 200 percent, but your losses may be 100 percent. These are large percentages simply because the initial investment is so low.

ORDERS

You can use just about any type of order for entering and exiting long puts. However, it is recommended that you use some type of limit order when trading options with little liquidity. (See Chapter 2 - The Fundamentals Of Options for more information on the types of orders.)

DECISION STRUCTURE

Selecting a Put

Selecting which put to buy requires an examination of expiration date, strike price, and price.

Expiration Date

The selection of the expiration date is largely dependent on when you expect the price of the underlying instrument to drop. If you believe that a decline in price is imminent, buy the nearby expiration. It will respond the most to the down-move, and provide the greatest leverage because it will have a higher delta than farther expirations. In addition, its time value will be less than that of farther expiration months and will therefore be less expensive while providing greater profits. Consider buying the farther expiration months if you are unsure when the market will make its move, or if you think the market may be steady but you want to make sure you don't miss the move. The relative prices are also important. You may want to pay a higher price for a farther month just to have more time for the trade to work. The extra time premium may be a cheap price to pay for several more months for the trade to work. However, most traders do not hold positions very long, and the extra price may be a waste of time.

Strike Price

Your market attitude determines which strike price to select. The more bearish you are, the lower the strike you should select. Puts with higher strike prices require a larger down-side move before they are profitable on the last day of trading. Puts with higher strike prices require smaller moves to the down-side before they are profitable at expiration. Once the low-strike put goes into the money, its percentage return skyrockets. The main reason is that the investment is so much lower than for higher strike prices. Nonetheless, the rule is that lower strike puts have a greater percentage return than higher strike calls *if they go sufficiently in the money.*

If you are very bearish on the underlying instrument, then buy out-of-the-money puts. The lowest strike price is the most bearish. This will give you the greatest profit potential on a percentage basis, though there is less chance of success because the market has to drop farther before the put is in the money. If you are less bearish and want a greater chance of success, buy in-the-money puts. The highest strike price is the least bearish choice. You will be cutting your potential percentage return, but you will have a greater chance of success because the intrinsic value of the in-the-money puts gives you an advantage.

In effect, the out-of-the-money put has fewer dollars to risk but a greater probability of loss. For example, the price of the underlying instrument could drop slightly. You could lose money by having an out-of-the-money option but still make money with an in-the-money option. In addition, the chances of an in-the-money option expiring worthless are less than for an out-of-the-money option.

You will be better off buying an in-the-money option if you are looking for a quick move because the higher delta will respond immediately to any price change in the underlying instrument. Out-of-the-money options will require a greater move in the underlying instrument to get the same dollar gain. The choice then becomes which of the two will give the greatest percentage return on the investment given your price expectation.

An out-of-the-money put will give you greater returns on large price moves of the underlying instrument, but the in-the-money put will provide superior returns if the underlying instrument only drops moderately.

Many investors buy out-of-the-money puts because they are less expensive. This is a poor reason to buy a put. If you have so few funds that you cannot afford in-the-money puts, then you are probably speculating needlessly and taking on too much risk.

Price

The price you pay for the put is the final consideration for selecting a put. Examining the factors that influence the price will determine if you are getting a good price, and will give further clues to how the price of your selected options will behave. The major factor to consider is the expected volatility. Occasionally, you should consider expected changes in interest rates and, in some cases, expected dividend payments. The point of examining the factors that influence prices is to discover options that are undervalued relative to your estimate of the fair value of the option.

Expected Volatility

The expected volatility is the most important factor affecting your estimate of the fair value, and has a major impact on the selection of an option. If the volatility is expected to increase, the price of the option will be expected to increase, all other things being equal. You will need to have an option evaluation service or computer program calculate the effect of an increase or decrease in volatility on the position.

A decrease in volatility will have an adverse effect on your position. You must carefully weigh the effects of a decline in volatility versus your expected price move in the underlying instrument. Once again, a computer program or service that details implied volatilities and the effect of changes in implied volatility on the option is extremely important. It is quite possible to get an expected move in the underlying instrument but lose money on the put because the volatility has declined.

A ramification of this is that you should select puts on the basis of the expected volatility versus their current price. For example, assume that two underlying instruments are trading for the same price, but one has a volatility three times that of the other. That means that the options on the first instrument will be priced significantly higher than those on the second instrument. If the options on the first instrument are priced below a level that compensates for the greater volatility, it represents a better deal than the second option.

Systematic Put Selection

Most people view the selection of puts as entirely derived from their projections of the price of the underlying instrument. This is certainly valid. But you can also examine the risk/reward of various puts first without looking at the merits of the underlying instrument. One method is to list puts in various rankings. For example, you could list all puts by their risk/reward characteristics given certain market moves. Note that you could examine all flavors of options, from OEX to soybeans, and apply the same criteria. Or you could focus on just those options in a group that you have selected through other means.

For example, suppose you think the computer industry stocks will go up in price but you don't know which stock or option to buy because you don't pick specific stocks. You could rank the options of the computer stocks by criteria that fit your trading style.

Consider ranking the options by a risk/reward ratio. First, pick a time horizon. For example, you look for the move to lower prices to occur over the coming three months. Assume that each stock in the industry group will move either up or down by the amount of the implied volatility. Alternately, assume that they will move higher or lower by your expected volatility. Note that we are assuming that the price could move both up and down, even though we are examining these particular stocks because we think they will slump. We do this so we may estimate their prices after both rises and falls so that we may estimate the reward from the expected price decline and the risk if we are wrong.

Thus, we take the implied or estimated volatility for each stock and estimate the price of the options given a price movement equal to the volatility during the time period, and then divide the resulting bullish option price by the bearish option price. The resulting ratio will give an excellent guide to the relative risk and reward of holding various options.

If the Price of the Underlying Instrument Rises

There are four possible strategies. First, if you are now bullish, liquidate the trade. The other three strategies are for use only if you are still bearish.

The first strategy is to hold your current position. This is often the best choice if there is little premium left, and therefore little dollar risk in holding the position. However, it is not a good strategy if there is little time before expiration, and if the market would have to drop substantially to hit your break-even point.

The second choice is rolling up. This strategy entails selling two of your current puts, and buying a put with a higher strike price. Your position will then be long one put with a higher strike price and short one put with your original strike price. In effect, you have rolled out of your long put position into a bear put spread (see Chapter 13 - Bear Spreads for more details). One critical factor is to try to buy the higher strike price for about the same price as the combined prices of the two puts you sold. For example, you will try to buy the OEX 160 calls at 5 if you can sell the two OEX 150 puts for 2 1/2 each.

This strategy does not require the sharp drop in the underlying instrument to make money. It therefore puts you in a better position to gain. The sacrifice is that the profit potential is reduced significantly. The net result is that the break-even point is lowered, the dollar risk stays about the same, but the maximum profit potential is also reduced. Another way to look at it is that the chance of success has improved, but the return from that success has been reduced.

Another strategy for holders of intermediate- or long-term puts is to sell a near-term put. For example, you are holding the OEX July 150 put and the price of the underlying index rises. You could sell an OEX April 150 put, creating a calendar spread (see Chapter 15 - Calendar Spreads for more details). Basically, you are trying to capture the time premium on the near put as a method of lowering the cost of the far put. This strategy is particularly attractive if the near put is about to expire and the time premium is decaying rapidly. Then, if the underlying instrument drops, you will still have the original put, but at a lower price.

Investors must be very cautious when using this strategy, however, because they have initiated a bullish position. A sharp rally in the underlying instrument while you are holding the short near put will probably create more losses in the near put than profits in the far put. Thus, you should be very sure that the market will not plunge lower over the near term.

If the Price of the Underlying Instrument Drops

If you are now bullish, liquidate the trade and take your profits.

You have several choices if you are still bearish:

1. Sell a lower strike and hold your existing put.
2. Sell your existing position and buy a lower strike.
3. Hold your existing put.

The first choice turns your long put into a bear put spread. This strategy costs nothing except the extra commission, though you may need to post additional margin, depending on the option. You will need to have a margin account if you are going to do this with stock options. You have essentially locked in your profit, but have retained more profit opportunity. This strategy will be the best if the market only slips a little more or is stable. The bear put strategy will have the worst performance if the market plummets. It's not that you will lose money, but that the profits will not be as high as with the two other strategies. The profit potential, though, is reduced to the difference between the strike prices. For example, you bought an OEX 150 put and the price of the underlying index has dipped. You could sell the OEX 130 put, lock in your profit, and retain the possibility of a further profit of 20 points, the difference between the 2 strike prices. (See Chapter 13 - Bear Spreads for more details on the ramifications of this strategy.)

The most aggressive approach, called rolling down, is to liquidate your current position and buy another put but at a lower strike price. This strategy is best if you are very bearish. Note, though, that the market must slide to below the new break-even point for you to make money on the new position. Thus, a stable or even slightly lower market will cause this strategy to be the worst of the three. For example, assume you bought an OEX 150 put at 5, it currently trades at 15, and that the OEX 130 calls are trading for 3. You could liquidate the OEX 150s, take the 10-point profit, and invest 3 in the OEX 130 calls. Notice that you have taken out the money you initially invested and are now using only your profits to invest with.

The third strategy is to hold your existing position. This strategy is best if you are looking for a moderate move lower, but is the worst of the three if the market climbs above the original break-even point. Note that this is the riskiest of the three strategies because it is the only one that could produce a loss on the whole series of transactions. For example, you bought the OEX 150 puts at 5 and they have gone to 15. The other two strategies lock in some of the profit at this point. Holding the existing position will lose money if the price of the OEX pops above the break-even point.

Further changes in the risk/reward situation can be accomplished by changing the number of contracts used in each strategy. For example, you could sell twice as many puts as you have long puts in the bear put strategy. This is obviously a more bullish strategy than writing the same number of puts as you originally bought. The price of the underlying instrument could now probably climb, and you would still make a profit. Or how about buying twice as many puts when you roll down? You are now taking a much more bearish stance in the market.

If the Option is About to Expire

Another consideration is the time left on the position. Time decay accelerates near option expiration. This makes holding options less attractive. Your choices are the same as initiating a new trade. The additional wrinkle is that time decay is a more important consideration near expiration. In general, if you are still bearish, you should roll forward into the next expiration month as a tactic to reduce the impact of the time decay. If you are now bullish, liquidate the trade before all the time premium decays.

Another decision is whether or not to exercise. You will never want to exercise if the option has any time premium. This is because the exercise of the option will cause you to lose the remaining time premium.

In general, it is unwise to exercise if there is a cost to the exercise process. For example, it costs extra commissions to exercise a stock option because commissions must be paid on the short sale of the stock. On the other hand, there is automatic exercise of many futures options where the cost is neglible. In most cases, you are better off buying back the put if the premium is greater than the cost of commissions.

6

Naked Call Writing

STRATEGY

Naked call writing is selling a call without owning the underlying instrument. If your portfolio consisted of only a short OEX call, you would be short a naked call.

Naked call writing is a bearish strategy. Call writers want the price of the underlying instrument to drop so they may buy back the call at a lower price. The best situation for a naked call writer is for the price of the underlying instrument to fall below the call's strike price at expiration, thus rendering the call worthless. The naked call writer will have captured all of the premium as profit.

Notice that the naked call write has a limited profit potential, yet unlimited loss potential. However, some studies have suggested that over 75 percent of options expire worthless.

The choice between shorting a naked call or the underlying instrument is based on several criteria. Let's look first at the situation at expiration. In terms of price action, the naked call is superior if the price of the underlying instrument is at the break-even point (discussed below) down to the strike price minus the call premium. Below that level, the short underlying instrument is superior. In other words, a very bearish outlook is better served by shorting the underlying instrument, whereas a less bearish outlook is better served by selling the naked call.

The situation before expiration is different. If you intend to actively manage your naked calls, then selling naked calls can be as attractive as short selling the underlying instrument. The use of naked call writes as an attractive substitute for short selling the underlying instrument requires active management to mitigate, though not eliminate, the additional risk. The form of the active management is detailed throughout the rest of this chapter.

One advantage of selling a call is that you are not liable for dividend or interest payments, if applicable. In fact, the payment of dividends or interest causes the call to drop in value an equivalent amount and thus enhances the profitability.

Another advantage of the naked call is that time is on the side of the naked call seller. As the option nears expiration, the time premium on the call evaporates and reduces the value of the call.

EQUIVALENT STRATEGY

An essentially equivalent strategy can be created by selling the underlying instrument and selling a put. It is unlikely that you will want to sell the instrument and sell the put if you can simply sell the call. Selling the call is easier to execute and will cost less in commissions.

The only time the equivalent strategy makes sense is if you already have one of the two legs on and want to change the character of the trade. Suppose you are very bearish and sell the underlying instrument. Later, you decide the market is not as bearish and may even rebound temporarily. This is the type of situation where you may initiate a synthetic naked call write.

RISK/REWARD

Net Investment

The net investment is the margin required by the broker to carry the position. Each exchange has different rules for devising the margin requirements for the naked call write, and each broker can then boost the margin to a higher level than specified by the exchanges.

Break-even Point

The break-even point at expiration is equal to the strike price plus the call premium. For example, if the strike is $50 and the call premium is $3, the underlying instrument cannot be higher than $53 at the expiration of the call.

The break-even point prior to expiration is the same as the break-even point at expiration, assuming that other pricing variables, such as the implied volatility and the risk-free rate, have not changed in the meantime.

Profit Potential

The maximum profit potential is the call premium received when the call is sold. This will occur only if the price of the underlying instrument is less than the strike price at expiration. The reason that the maximum profit potential is only reached at expiration is that the option will always have a time premium up to the last minutes of trading. You therefore have to let the option expire before the maximum profit potential can be reached.

The naked call will also profit at expiration if the price of the underlying instrument lies between the strike price and the strike price plus the call premium. The rule in this case is: The profit equals the call premium plus the strike price minus the price of the underlying instrument.

Before expiration, the naked call will be making money if the price of the underlying instrument has dropped since the naked call write was initiated. The profit (or loss) can be estimated by the delta of the option. For example, if you sold an option for $5 with a delta of .50, the option will be close to $3 if the price of the underlying instrument has fallen $4. Note that deltas change as the price and implied volatility change. This means that you can only estimate the future value of the option, not pinpoint it precisely.

A drop in implied volatility can increase profits. This occurs because the price of an option is largely determined by the implied volatility. A reduction in the implied volatility will reduce the value of the options, thus creating a more profitable situation for you. In fact, you can make money on a naked call if the implied volatility drops and the price of the underlying instrument stays the same. You need an options valuation model to determine the effect of the shift.

Potential risk

The risk in holding a naked option is unlimited. As a practical matter, of course, you should be taking defensive measures before losses climb out of sight. The risk is that the price of the underlying instrument will rally while you are short the call. The dollar risk can be estimated by multiplying the option delta times the price change of the underlying instrument. For example, you will lose $3 if the delta is .30 and the underlying instrument rallies $10.

One risk is that the option will be assigned before you wish to exit the trade. This risk is largely controlled by your selection of strike price. An in-the-money option has a chance of early exercise, while an out-of-the-money option has very little chance of early exercise.

An increase in volatility will hurt your position because it will increase the value of the option. For example, assume an at-the-money option on a $50 instrument with 90 days to expiration and implied volatility of 10 percent. This option will be worth about .98. An increase in implied volatility to 15 percent will boost the price of the option to $1.47 without any change in the price of the underlying instrument.

DECISION STRUCTURE

Selection

Market outlook is critical to the selection of the option to write. The more bearish you are the lower the strike price you will select. The reasons for this are that the delta will be higher for a lower strike price than for a higher strike, and that the premium is higher, thus affording greater profit potential. A more defensive posture is to sell at higher strike prices. An out-of-the-money option has less chance of being in-the-money at expiration than an in-the-money option.   The trade-off is that the premium and, hence, the profit potential, is less.

One strategy is to sell options that have a strike price higher than the implied volatility suggests as the range in the relevent time period.   For example, the Swiss franc is currently trading at 61.00, the implied volatility is 12 percent, and there are 3 months left to trade the option.   Implied volatility suggests that prices will trade in a range of 1.83 (3 percent times 61.00) above and below 61.00.   This suggests selecting a call 1.83 higher than the current market price, perhaps the 63.00 call.   A more conservative approach would be to sell a call even higher, perhaps twice the range suggested by the implied volatility.

Implied volatility has a major impact on the selection of the underlying instrument to write a call against.   The best strategy is to sell options that have a high implied volatility, looking for both prices and volatility to fall.   It is very helpful to keep a record or graph of the implied volatilities for the recent past.   This will provide a perspective on the volatility of the call you want to write. In general, you will want to write calls that have a high implied volatility rather than a low implied volatility.

Selling a call is a way of selling time premium. Selling calls is most attractive, all other things being equal, when there is little time left before expiration.   Time decay is limited in the first days after an option is listed.   As time progresses, the time decay accelerates, making selling options more attractive the more expiration approaches.

If the Price of the Underlying Instrument Drops

If you are no longer bearish, simply liquidate the trade and take your profits.

If you are still bearish, you have three possibilities. First, continue holding your existing position.   This can be a very attractive proposition if the call is out-of-the-money and there is little time left before expiration. This strategy is also suited to a market stance that is only slightly bearish.

A more bearish market stance would suggest rolling down to a lower strike price. This will give you more profit potential because the delta and the premium will be higher.

If the option is about to expire, you can roll forward. The selection of which option to roll forward into will be related to your market outlook. Note that you probably don't want to liquidate your existing call if the time premium is falling rapidly and there is little chance for the option to go in-the-money. In this circumstance, you may want to take a larger risk and sell options on the next expiration while still holding the nearby options. The reward is that you will capture the time premium on the nearby options while holding your longer term position in the farther contract. The risk is that the market will rally sharply, and you will lose money on both the nearby and farther options simultaneously.

If the Price of the Underlying Instrument Rises

If the market is moving against you and you look for it to continue to do so, liquidation of the position makes the most sense.

Another plan, if you have turned bullish, is to buy the underlying instrument. You will have converted the short call into a covered call write. The critical question is whether to buy an underlying instrument in the same quantity as the short call or in a delta neutral quantity. Using the same quantity is more bullish than placing positions in a delta neutral quantity. (See Chapter 7 - Covered Call Writing and Chapter 8 - Ratio Covered Call Writing for more details.)

If you think the rally is temporary, you could continue to hold your current position or roll up. Holding the current position is more aggressive than rolling up. The lower strike will have more risk and reward than the higher strike.

If the option is about to expire and you are still bearish, you can roll forward. The selection of which strike to sell will follow the guidelines outlined above. One decision you will need to make is whether to liquidate the current position and the attendant sharp decay in time premium, or sell the far options and hang onto the current position. The question comes down to your market outlook. Will the price rally more than the time decay? If so, roll forward. If not, hang onto the current position and sell the next expiration option.

7

Covered Call Writing

A. Strategy
B. Equivalent strategy
C. Risk/reward
D. Orders
E. Writing against instrument already owned
F. Physical location of underlying instrument
G. Decision structure
H. Write against a convertible security
I. Diversification of profit and protection

STRATEGY

Covered call writing is being long an underlying instrument and short a call on that instrument.

The list below shows the various calls available and the instruments that the call could be written against:

Stock Indexes

- Cash portfolio representative of the stock index
- Call with lower strike price and same expiration
- Long futures contract

Stocks

- Underlying stock
- Call with lower strike price and same expiration
- Convertible securities

Futures

- Cash instrument/commodity
- Futures contract
- Call with lower strike price and same expiration

Bull call spread is the name for writing a call against another call with a lower strike price. We will not go into further detail concerning bull call spreads in this chapter because they deserve their own chapter (see Chapter 12 - Bull Spreads).

The quantity represented by the number of calls sold is equal to the quantity of the underlying instrument. For example, covered call writing using options on Eastman Kodak will have one short call option for every long 100 shares. Another example is selling one Treasury-bond option against the purchase of one Treasury-bond futures contract. (Ratio call writing is the strategy of using differing quantities of the underlying instrument and call options, and is outlined in Chapter 8 - Ratio Covered Call Writing.)

There are three main reasons behind writing covered calls:

1. Partially hedge existing position against price decline.
2. Increase return on existing long position.
3. Furnish an opportunity for profit.

EQUIVALENT STRATEGY

Naked Put Write

The naked put write can be substituted in many cases for a covered call write, particularly with instruments that pay dividends or interest. There are several main considerations for deciding whether to naked put write or covered call write. The first is commissions. Commissions will be significantly higher for covered call writing than for naked put writing. The second consideration is the total return from the investment. A covered call write on stocks or debt instruments may have a dividend or interest payment that can boost the return beyond the higher cost of commissions. The third consideration is that you may already be long the underlying instrument so that covered writing may be the only practical action. The alternative would be to sell the underlying instrument and initiate a naked put write. It may be cheaper in commissions to simply sell the calls against the instrument than liquidate, and then start a new position from scratch.

A major difference between a naked put write and a covered call write is that the covered call write provides a measure of down-side protection but a naked put write does not. A naked put write is thus a more aggressive position.

RISK/REWARD

Maximum Profit Potential

The maximum profit potential is equal to the strike price of the option minus the underlying instrument price plus the price of the call.

Maximum profit potential = strike price - UI price + call price

Since calls can be written against a variety of underlying instruments, the transaction and carrying costs will vary. For example, a covered call program for stock indexes can have calls written against a portfolio of stocks, a long call with lower strike price, or a portfolio of convertible securities that relate to the stock portfolio underlying the stock index option.

Let's look at an example of the maximum profit potential. Suppose you want to enter into a covered call writing program using the OEX stock index against a portfolio of stocks that mimic the OEX. (The OEX is an index composed of 100 large NYSE stocks. It is possible to mimic the index by buying all the stocks in that index in the proper proportions.) If the underlying stock portfolio is bought for cash, carrying costs are only the dividends received on the portfolio. Margin costs must be subtracted if the portfolio is bought on margin. For example, assume the following:

A $1 million portfolio of stocks that mimic the OEX
Dividend yield = 5 percent
Strike price = 150
Stock index price = 149
Call price = 4
Transaction costs = $16,000
Broker loan rate = 12 percent
Hold the trade for three months

The maximum profit potential will be the strike price (150) minus the stock index price (149) plus the call price (4). The result is 5. Let's look at the actual transaction. You would hold 67 contracts of the OEX ($1 million divided by 149 equals 67 contracts, rounded off). Your profit is 5 times the 100 point value of the OEX times the 67 contracts. This equals a $33,500 profit.

Break-even Point and Down-side Protection

Covered call writing partially hedges both up and down price moves. Figure 7.1 shows the profit/loss diagram for a covered call at expiration. The short call limits the profit potential of the long underlying instrument, but buffers the long position from losses by the amount of the premium only.

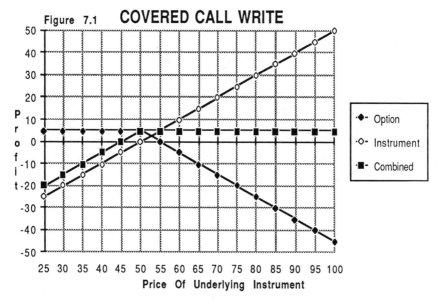

Figure 7.1   **COVERED CALL WRITE**

Losses may be reduced but not limited. Losses are reduced because you receive the call premium, which buffers you from the full value of a price decline. Covered calls show significant losses as the underlying instrument falls below the break-even point. The maximum theoretical risk occurs when the value of the underlying instrument falls to zero.

On the other hand, covered call writing does have limited profit potential. Figure 7.1 shows how the total profit is limited when the instrument price rises above the maximum gain level. At that point, gains in the underlying instrument are matched dollar for dollar with the losses in the short call at expiration.

The break-even point is critical for evaluating potential investments. The break-even point shows the amount of down-side protection that the covered call position provides. One advantage of covered call writing over many investments is that it is possible to reduce the break-even point to below the initial entry level.

The simple break-even point, in formula form, is:

Break-even point = UI price - call premium

For example, use the assumptions given above of a stock index price of 149 and a call premium of 4. The stock index price (149) minus the call premium (4) equals the break-even point (145).

Figure 7.2, opposite, shows the break-even point for this example. Note that you bought the stock index at 149, but you will not lose money unless the index is below 145 at the expiration of the option. For example, suppose the stock index is at 148 at expiration. This means that the call options will be worthless, but you will have the 4 that you received when you sold the option. However, you will have to pay the owner the difference between the current value of the stock index and the strike price, in this case 2. This leaves you with a 2 profit from the sale of the option minus the 1 loss on the purchase of the stock index, for a total profit of 1.

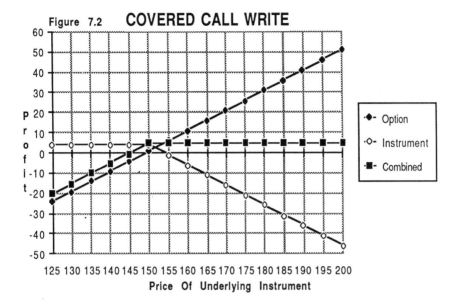

Figure 7.2 **COVERED CALL WRITE**

Price Of Underlying Instrument

You can lose money before the expiration of the contract if the price of the stock index declines. For example, suppose the stock index went to 145 the first day after initiating a covered call position. The value of the call will have dropped below its initial 4 price, but not enough to offset the decline in value of the stock increase, because the delta is less than 1.00. This occurs because the value of the call is composed mainly of time value rather than intrinsic value. The decline will be greater if the option is in the money because it will have more intrinsic value. Remember that the simple break-even point describes the situation only at the expiration of the option.

The break-even point is affected by the type of account and transaction. The trade can take place using cash or on margin. Margin, in this context, means borrowing money to buy more stock. Transaction costs for margin trades will be more than for cash trades. Additional carrying costs for trades on margin include the financing for the additional stock. The carrying cost for a cash transaction will only be the opportunity cost.

The break-even point outlined above describes the situation at expiration only. Before then, the break-even point changes with time. The break-even point on the first day in the trade is the entry level. Over time, the break-even point will drop below the entry level. The time value of the call decays, creating the profits that reduce the break-even point. This shows that a covered call program can stack the odds in your favor.

The down-side protection specified by the break-even point is affected by the strike price of the call. A covered call using a lower strike price write will have greater down-side protection than using a higher strike price. The greater premium income provides greater down-side protection.

Net Investment Required

The net investment required for a stock trade in a cash account is the money necessary for purchase of the underlying instrument. The sale of the call is a credit to your account, though you must keep the money in your account. Table 7.1 shows an example of selling an April Widget 65 call at $4 against stock bought at $62.

Table 7.1. Simple net investment required

Cost of stock	$6200
Minus option premium received	(400)
	____
Net investment required	$5800

The net investment required for a margin account is the capital for the leveraged purchase of the underlying stock. The sale of the call is a credit to your account in this case as well.

The investment for a covered write in futures is the premium of the option (marked to the market) plus the greater of: the underlying futures margin minus one-half of the amount that the option is in-the-money, or one-half the amount of the underlying futures margin.

The Investment Return

There are two major ways to calculate the return on your investment. Each presents a different perspective on the proposed trade. Both should be examined before initiating a position.

Return if Exercised

The return if exercised is the return on the investment if the underlying instrument is called away. The return if exercised depends on the type of option and the price action after trade entry. An out-of-the-money option must have the underlying instrument rise to above the strike price, or there is no return if exercised. This is because the option will not be exercised if it is out-of-the-money, and thus no return if exercised. An in-the-money covered write only requires the instrument price to remain unchanged. You will receive the return if exercised for an in-the-money covered write even if the instrument price is unchanged. The return if exercised is the same as the return if unchanged for an in-the-money write (see Return if Unchanged on p. 88). Remember that the deeper the option is in-the-money, the higher the probability that the return if exercised will actually be attained. Comparing the relative merits of different strike prices used in covered writes requires an assumption about the direction of prices.

Let's look at an example, an out-of-the-money covered write. We'll continue the example started in Table 7.1. You are selling an April Widget 65 call at $4 against your long 100 shares at $62. The return if exercised can be calculated after the net investment required is known. Table 7.1 shows the net investment required and Table 7.2 shows the return if exercised.

Table 7.2.   Return if exercised

Proceeds from stock sale	$6500
Minus net investment	(5800)
Net profit	$700
Return if exercised = 700/5800 = 12%	

The return if exercised in this example is 12 percent. You should also look at the annualized return for better comparison with other investments. Suppose you held the Widget covered call position for three months. Your annualized return would be 48 percent (12 percent return for 3 months is equivalent to 48 percent return for one year).

Return if Unchanged

The return if unchanged is the return on your investment if there is no change in the price of the underlying instrument from date of entry to expiration. This method of calculation return has a major advantage over the return if exercised; it makes no assumption about future prices. It gives a closer approximation of the return you should expect. The return if unchanged is the same as the return if exercised for an in-the-money write (see Return if Exercised on p. 87).

Table 7.3   Simple return if unchanged

Proceeds from stock sale	$6200
Minus net investment required	(5800)
Net profit	$400
Return if unchanged = 400/5800 = 6.9%	

Additional Income

You may receive additional income if you have the opportunity to compound some of the income received during the covered call position. For example, you may receive dividends or interest from your covered call before the end of the trade. These payments can be reinvested and compounded. However, this will only be a minor source of additional revenue, and will not likely be a factor in your decision to invest in a particular program.

ORDERS

It is usually best to enter covered call writes as a contingent order, sometimes called a net covered writing order. This instructs the broker to simultaneously execute the purchase of the underlying instrument and the sale of the call at a net price. Use these orders for both entering.and exiting covered writes. Some brokers may have a minimum order size for accepting these orders.

Order entry is important because almost all options are traded on a different exchange than the underlying instrument. The only major exception is options on futures, where the option is traded in the pit next to the instrument. For example, cattle options are traded just a few feet away from the cattle futures pit, but IBM stock is traded around the world, but not at the CBOE, where the option is traded.

The separation of the options exchange and the exchange where the underlying instrument is sold makes it more expensive and awkward to execute orders. The brokerage house will not guarantee that the contingency or net covered call write orders will be filled. They will try to fill the order at the market bids and asks. The broker may even try to leg into the trade. However, the broker will not fill the order if the risk of loss is too high.

Unfortunately, you may sometimes have to use orders other than contingency orders. This mainly occurs when the underlying instrument and the option trade on different exchanges.

The alternative to the contingency order is the market order. This guarantees a fill, but may be at prices that are unacceptable; your expected returns may be significantly altered. You are looking for a particular return when writing calls. Any return less than expected may induce you to discard the trade. This means you should always use contingency orders even if you cannot initiate a position. At least you will get the expected price and return.

The use of the net or contingency order has one wrinkle. The order is placed by giving the net price of the covered call. For example, you may see a good opportunity by doing a covered call write on 100 shares of General Widget. The stock is currently trading at $62 and the option is at $4. The net price you want is $58 ($62 - $4 = $58). Although unlikely, the net order could be filled at $63 and $5, or $59 and $1. Your analysis has been predicated on getting $62 and $4. In most cases, you will get a quote on the covered write, and your order will be filled close enough to that quote so it doesn't substantially change the outcome of the trade. In a fast moving market, however, the fill on the order could change the risk and return of the trade. A fill at $59 and $1 gives very little down-side protection, but more profit potential, while the fill at $63 and $5 gives greater protection but less potential. In addition, the return if exercised remains stable but the return if unchanged and the break-even point have changed dramatically.

Another subtle difference in the fills is the commissions. The fill at $63 and $5 will have higher commissions than the one at $59 and $1, because commissions are usually charged on the value of the transaction for stock options. Once again, your fills will usually be very close to your desired price, and the difference in commissions will be negligible.

WRITING AGAINST INSTRUMENT ALREADY OWNED

Covered call writing profits are relatively small, and the costs of trading need to be carefully monitored. Writing calls against your existing portfolio may increase the yield of covered call writing because you have already paid the commission to enter the underlying instrument. You do not have to pay a commission to buy the underlying instrument. This can have a large percentage impact on your return. Be sure to compare the returns of various writes after taking into account the commission savings of using an underlying instrument you already own. The returns of selling against what you already own will often be greater than starting a trade from scratch because of the commission savings.

PHYSICAL LOCATION OF UNDERLYING INSTRUMENT

The physical location of the underlying instrument affects the net investment required. In the examples above, it was assumed the underlying instrument was on deposit with the same broker selling your calls. No additional margin deposit is required if you write calls against an underlying instrument that is being carried by the same broker. For example, you may write a sugar call against a long sugar futures position without investing any further money if the futures contract is being carried with the same broker who is executing the short call. In most cases, you will be initiating the long and short at the same time; the short call will not increase your gross investment.

This does not apply if the underlying instrument and the call are traded on two different exchanges. Then, each side of the write must have the full requirement even if they are traded with the same broker.

However, you may have stock that you cannot or will not deposit with a broker. There are ways that you can still write calls without increased investment. You may deposit the stock with a bank, which will issue an escrow receipt or letter of guarantee to the brokerage house. The brokerage house must approve the bank before accepting the letter of guarantee, and not all brokers accept guarantees. In addition, the bank will charge you for the letter of guarantee. This generally makes it too expensive for small traders.

Another method is to deposit your stock with a bank that is a member of the Depository Trust Corporation (DTC). The DTC guarantees to the Options Clearing Corporation (OCC) that it will deliver the stock if the short call is assigned. This is the method used by most institutional covered writers. The cost may be zero, but only a few banks are members, and they tend to be located in major cities.

DECISION STRUCTURE

The decision structure for a covered call program has the usual selection and two follow-up strategies. However, the selection of a covered call is dependent on the rationale behind the trade. Each reason has a unique selection structure. One factor affects all three strategies.

A change in implied volatility will affect the price of the written call. Your preference should be to write options that have a high implied volatility, with you expecting declining volatility. The worst circumstance would be to write a call with low implied volatility with the expectation of increasing volatility.

What Is Your Strategy?

Now, let's take a look at the three main reasons behind covered call writing:

1. Partially hedge existing position against price decline
2. Increase return on existing long position
3. Furnish an opportunity for profit

Hedge Existing Position

The first strategy is to write a call against an instrument you think is going to drop in price near term, but will move higher long term. The idea is that the option premium will protect you against the price drop without having to post any additional funds. Besides that, you may make a little money on the decay of the time value. However, remember that selling a call may mean that you will have to give up your long position if the call is exercised. You may have protected a position you will no longer have. In fact, the short call will protect the instrument price against a small price drop, but the strategy falls apart if the market rallies. Your instrument will be called away if the call is exercised. You wanted to carry the instrument until a particular time, but the market took it away early. To partially protect against this, use an option that doesn't expire until after you want to liquidate the short call. Look at other hedge strategies, such as buying puts (see Chapter 5 - Buy A Put).

This strategy implies the sale of an in-the-money call to provide protection. Select the quantity of the in-the-money call that has a delta that will cover the expected price drop. Remember, very in-the-money calls often have poor liquidity, and entering and exiting the short call may be difficult.

Be sure to have the proper number of short options. Find the option's delta to construct a delta neutral position to make sure you have enough calls to provide adequate protection.

Increase Return

The second strategy is to increase return on an existing position. Where do you think the price of the underlying instrument is going? If you are long-term bearish, get out of the underlying instrument and invest in something else. If you are bullish, treat the covered call write as a separate trade and follow the decision outlined in the section below. When you write a call against an existing position, you are no longer in that existing position. Many investors psychologically cling to the long position and do not realize that the sale of the call means that they have liquidated a long position and simultaneously initiated a covered call write. These are two separate trades with differing risk/reward characteristics and decision structures.

Selling a call is a powerful way to increase returns on an underlying instrument that has a predetermined sell point. Selling a call at the strike price that corresponds to the sell point increases your returns by the amount of the premium, while reducing the risk. Selling a call is essentially preselling your long instrument. When the instrument rises to your target price, the call buyer may call away your instrument. The critical problem is identifying a valid target sale price.

It is a problem when you have an objective that is above the highest strike price, or when the premium for the strike price at your target is very low. A premium worth only $50 is not high enough to sell. It is probably a better strategy in this case to sell a strike price close to the current instrument price and continually roll up by selling additional calls as the instrument price climbs to your objective. Selling additional calls essentially changes this from a covered call to a ratio covered call. It is essential that you roll up for a credit; otherwise, you are not increasing your returns.

Furnish Opportunity for Profit

First determine your market attitude. A stable market outlook is the best time to sell calls if premiums are high. Don't write calls if you are bearish on the underlying instrument. If you are very bullish on the underlying instrument, sell out-of-the-money calls (or wait until later to sell the call). This will give you the greatest profit potential, although you will give up some down-side protection. An alternative strategy for the very bullish is to not sell as many options as underlying instruments. For example, sell 3 calls against your 400 shares of United Widget. If risk protection is more important, sell in-the-money calls. You will be cutting your potential return, but you won't have as great a risk of loss as selling out-of-the-money calls. Be careful that you are not cutting your potential return to such a low level that it doesn't compensate for the risk. Your subjective criterion of risk versus profit potential, combined with the range of available in-the-money and out-of-the-money options, gives you the ability to fine-tune your covered call program.

You need to consider at least three statistics when covered call writing: break-even point, return if exercised, and return if unchanged. Annualize the return figures to make them easier to compare with each other and other covered writes. Comparing annualized returns is useful, but those yields are not engraved in stone. You must evaluate the probability of those returns being achieved. You may find one covered call with an annualized return if unchanged of 40 percent and another one of only 20 percent, but the second covered write is a better investment if your estimation of the chance of success for the first one is only 30 percent, while the chance for the second write is 80 percent.

Another consideration is the down-side protection of the proposed trade. You need to find the right combination of profit potential with risk protection. Filter the universe of potential writes to those that provide the minimum amount of desired protection.

If the Price of the Underlying Instrument Drops

There are two choices. The first is to liquidate the trade. This is the preferred choice if you are now very bearish and think the price of the underlying instrument will never move back above your break-even point.

The second choice, rolling down, can provide additional protection while keeping the possibility of profit should the market move back up. It is called rolling down because you buy back the original call and sell a call with a lower strike price as the price of the underlying instrument moves lower. The additional premium provides additional down-side protection, though profit potential becomes more limited. If the price of the underlying instrument continues down and you keep selling calls, you may reach a point of locking in a loss. The question then becomes: Is the loss from rolling down bigger than the loss of letting my current position ride? Remember, you are in effect initiating a new position, so the criteria for entering a new position apply.

For example, you are long widget futures at 190 and short a June 180 call at 18. Your down-side protection extends down to 172 (excluding transaction and carrying costs). Two weeks later the government releases its widget crop report that shows large plantings of widgets. The price of widgets declines to $172, while the June 180 call drops to $2 and the 160 call is trading for $15. You've lost two points on your position and have reached the break-even point. The price of widgets will have to be unchanged

for you to split even. You have little protection left in your June
180 call, but you can increase protection by selling the June 160 call
and buying back the June 180 call.

After this transaction, you have down-side protection to $149
because you sold a net premium of $13 (the price of the June 160
call, $15, minus the price of the June 180 call, $2). The premium
collected is subtracted from the original break-even point to derive
the new break-even point. Notice you will make 13 points at the
current level if the widget price is unchanged. Rolling down
gained additional protection and a chance to make money at the
lower level. If you stuck with the original position, you would
have made only the 2 points remaining on the June 180 call.

The problem with rolling down is that you are reducing your profit
potential. You have agreed to have your widget future called away
at $160 rather than at $180. Table 7.4 shows the results of the
original write and the rolled down position, while Figure 7.3 shows
the option chart for the same two strategies. You have, in effect,
swapped additional protection for reduced profit protection.

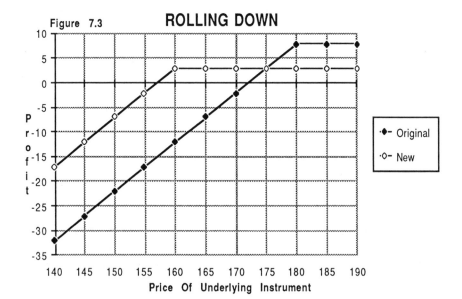

Table 7.4. Profit/loss - rolling down

Price at expiration	Original write	Rolled down position
140	-32	-17
150	-22	-7
160	-12	3
170	-2	3
172	0	3
180	8	3
190	8	3

The key is when, if ever, to roll down. This is a market timing decision. Liquidate the trade if you have turned bearish. If you are still bullish, the point to roll down might be at the original break-even point, a technical support point, or a money management point.

The real problem arises when the price drops quickly, you don't respond quickly enough, and the market presents you with only an opportunity to roll down and lock in a loss. This is more likely with out-of-the-money writes because they provide less down-side protection. The choice may simply be to lock in a small loss rather than carry the risk of a much larger loss. Be alert to negative price moves and have a plan for rolling down firmly in place before initiating the original write.

There are three other ways to roll down. First, roll down part of your position and keep part in the original call. This increases your down-side protection but gives higher profit potential than rolling down the entire position.

The second way to roll down is to keep the original write, then write another call at the lower strike price. This becomes, in effect, a ratio write with two strike prices. You will be short two calls against one long underlying instrument. (See Chapter 8 - Ratio

Covered Call Writing for more details on the strategic implications and the risk/reward characteristics.)

The third way is to roll down and forward. In other words, buy back your original call and sell a call at a lower strike price and in the next expiration month. This has the advantage/disadvantage of giving more time for your trade to either work or backfire. One possibility is to partially roll down and forward. Keep some of your original write, and roll down and forward some into the next expiration month. Note that rolling down and forward restricts the maximum profit potential for a longer period of time.

If the Price of the Underlying Instrument Rises

The first choice is to liquidate the trade and take the profit you had planned. This is particularly attractive if the return comes quickly. There are two other possibilities: letting the instrument be called away, and rolling up.

The instrument will likely be called away from you if the price of the underlying instrument rises above the strike price. This is simply another way of liquidating the trade. When the call is exercised, you will have disposed of the call and the underlying instrument at the same time (unless you decide to hold the underlying instrument and acquire another to deliver). You will receive the return if exercised on the trade.

In many cases, it is better to roll forward rather that have the underlying instrument called away. You will be saving commissions and, as was pointed out above, this can increase the return significantly. You will certainly want to roll forward if there is not much time premium left and you are still bullish or neutral.

Writing a futures option on a cash market position presents a further step in the analysis. In this case you may have the call exercised and be short a futures contract against the still-existing cash market position. For example, you write a Treasury-bond futures option against your cash position of a 7 1/4 percent long bond. Your call is exercised and you are left holding a short bond futures position. You can hold the short futures and long bond position, liquidate the futures and hold the long bond, or liquidate both.

Your decision will be first based on your market outlook. A bearish outlook would suggest liquidation of both in most cases. A bullish outlook would suggest liquidating the futures and holding onto the long bond.

If the short futures position was delivered to you at a price that was higher than you felt was reasonable, you may want to hold the long bond/short futures position until the price relationship between them moves back into line with your analysis. Remember, the long bond/short futures should be considered a new trade, not an extension of the covered call write.

Another alternative if the underlying instrument price rises is to roll up. This means writing more calls at higher strike prices as the price of the underlying instrument rises, while buying back the original short call. The key is market timing. You should keep writing calls as the market moves higher but not to the point where the price begins to drop.

Rolling up increases the maximum profit potential at the expense of the break-even point. Whereas rolling down is a credit transaction and you receive cash, rolling up is a debit transaction and you must pay additional cash. The break-even point is raised by the amount of the debit. However, you could combine the rolling up with rolling forward to the next expiration month as a potential tactic to reduce the debit. Let's look at an example of a price rally, starting with the covered call described in the rolling down section above. Now the widget futures contract is up to $200, the June 180 call sells for $25, and the June 220 call sells for $8. The roll-up will cost you $17, buying the June 180 at $25 and selling the June 220 at $8. Table 7.5 shows the new profit/loss picture, and Figure 7.4 shows the results of the two tactics.

Table 7.5. - Profit/loss - Rolling up

Price at expiration	Original write	Rolled up position
160	-12	-32
170	-2	-22
180	8	-12
190	8	-2
200	8	8
210	8	18
220	8	28
230	8	28

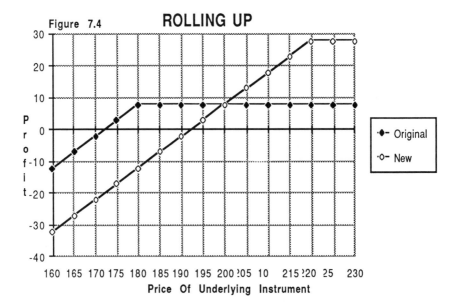

Figure 7.4 — ROLLING UP

Price Of Underlying Instrument

If the Option Is About to Expire

You are faced with several decisions. The time premium will have essentially vanished. There is no desirability to holding a short call if the time premium is gone. You should either liquidate the trade or roll forward and/or up. The decision is largely based on your market expectation. If your covered call position is profitable, you need to ask if your attitude on the market is bullish or bearish. If you are bullish, roll forward into the next expiring option month if the premium levels are attractive. You are initiating a new position, so the criteria for entering a new position apply. For example, you need to decide if an in-the-money or out-of-the-money call is appropriate.

A criterion for determining if you should roll forward is the return per day. However, it is only applicable for rolling forward into the same strike price. For example, you may be able to make $435 for the 23 days left on your current write, but $1919 on a write on the next expiration month that expires in 83 days. Your return per day on the current write is $18.91 (435/23 = 18.91), while the write on the next expiration month returns $23.12 (1919/83 = 23.12).

You should probably liquidate the trade if you are bearish. It is rarely wise to carry a covered call when you are bearish unless you are expecting a slight and temporary dip in the market. You can always write another call on the next expiration cycle when the dip is over.

If the option is about to expire and your total position is unprofitable, you have a couple of alternatives: Liquidate the trade unless you see an imminent market turnaround. If you are still bullish, you could roll forward and down.

WRITE AGAINST A CONVERTIBLE SECURITY

It is often more profitable to write calls against convertible securities. The most common convertible security is the convertible bond, though convertible preferreds and warrants are also candidates.

It is important to know the number of shares that the convertible converts into. You can then compute the correct number of options and convertibles to use. For example, a convertible bond may be converted to 20 shares of stock. You will need to own 5 bonds for every 1 call representing 100 shares that you sell. You will also need to know the yield on the convertible, and the margin requirements if you intend to finance the purchase. Let's compare examples of writing against a convertible and the underlying common.

International Business Widgets (IBW) has a convertible bond selling for 123 3/4, the stock is at 151 1/2, and the IBW May 155 calls are selling for 4 3/8. Each bond is convertible into 6.5 shares. This means that 200 bonds will give 1300 shares after conversion. Tables 7.6-7.11 show the results of writing against the common versus writing against the cash. Assume no financing costs and that you will hold the write for one month.

Table 7.6.   Net investment required - common

Cost of stock	$196,950
Plus stock commissions	1300
Minus options premium received	(5,688)
Plus options commissions	390
Net investment required	$192,952

Table 7.7.   Return if exercised - common

Proceeds from stock sale	$201,500
Minus stock commissions	(1300)
Plus dividends (.2%)	395
Minus net investment required	(192,952)
Net profit	$7,643

Return if exercised = 7,643/192,952 = 3.96% (47.53% annualized)

Table 7.8.   Return if unchanged - common

Proceeds from stock sale	$196,950
Minus stock commissions	(1300)
Plus dividends (.2%)	395
Minus net investment required	(192,952)
Net profit	$3093

Return if exercised = 3,093/192,952 = 1.60% (19.24% annualized)

Table 7.9.   Net investment required - convertible

Cost of bonds	$247,500
Minus options premium received	(5,688)
Plus options commissions	390
Net investment required	$242,202

Table 7.10.   Return if exercised - convertible

Proceeds from bond sale	$253,218
Plus coupon yield (7 7/8% coupon)	1312
Minus net investment required	(242,202)
Net profit	$12,328

Return if exercised = 12,328/242,202 = 5.09% (61.10% annualized)

Table 7.11.   Return if unchanged - convertible

Proceeds from bond sale	$247,500
Plus coupon yield (7 7/8% coupon)	1312
Minus net investment required	(242,202)
Net profit	$6,610

Return if exercised = 6,610/242,202 = 2.73% (32.70% annualized)

The net result is that you will have to invest more with the convertible, but your returns are likely to be higher. The convertible return if exercised is 61.10 percent versus 47.53 percent for the common. The convertible return if unchanged is 32.70 percent, versus 19.2 percent for the common.

It should be noted that the return if exercised is not as precise for the convertible as it is for the common. The example above assumed that the premium of the convertible price to the exercise price of the convertible was stable. In this example, there was a 22 percent premium for buying the convertible over the common. The return to exercise can be more or less for the convertible, because the premium may expand or contract.

The trickiest part of using a convertible instead of a stock is assignment if the call is exercised. There are two choices. The first is to convert the convertible into common stock and deliver the stock to the call buyer. This is virtually never a good idea because you will be losing the premium on the convertible. The second and practical choice is to sell the convertible and buy the stock to deliver.

Another concern is to find out whether the convertible is callable and, if so, what the terms are. Your strategy could be destroyed if the convertible is called away and you have to end the covered call prematurely.

DIVERSIFICATION OF PROFIT AND PROTECTION

The goal of your covered call writing is to find covered calls that provide the right combination of profit potential and risk protection. The problem is that the maximum profit potential comes from writing out-of-the-money calls, while the best protection comes from writing in-the-money calls. Another problem with writing only one type of option is that you are committed to just one strategy, and the potential for the strategy to fail is relatively high. However, you can diversify your portfolio of covered calls by using multiple strike prices. A combination of in-the-money and out-of-the-money options may provide a better balance of profit potential and risk protection. There will be a greater chance of achieving the expected results because you have diversified the potential risks and rewards across a broader array of strike prices.

Another way to increase the chances of achieving your expected return is to diversify through time. You can write calls at the same strike price in different expiration months. For example, you could write the April and July 85 Amalgamated Widget calls.

Combining these two techniques adds another dimension to your strategy. You can fine-tune the write program according to your expectations of future prices. For example, you may think that

Widget and Associates will be at $25 by April and $35 by July. You could write two out-of-the-money calls: an April 25 and a July 35. Alternately, you could write an in-the-money call at the nearest expiration to provide protection now but write an out-of-the-money call in the next expiration month to provide greater profit potential.

8

Ratio Covered
Call Writing

STRATEGY

Ratio covered call writing is being long an underlying instrument and short more calls on that instrument than you have of that instrument. For instance, you could be long 100 shares of Xerox and short two calls.

The main rationale for a ratio covered call write is to capture the time premium of the short calls. This is accomplished by buying the underlying instrument and selling enough calls to create a delta neutral position. This means that the sum of the deltas of the short calls will be equal to the delta of the long underlying instrument. For instance, you buy 100 shares of AT&T at 25 and sell 2 AT&T 25 options with deltas of .50 each. The delta on the long stock is 1.00, so you need to sell options that have a total delta of 1.00. In this case, you need to sell two options, because their deltas were .50.

Note that you have initiated a position that has a delta of zero. This means that you have no market exposure. This shows that a delta neutral ratio covered call write is a neutral strategy. You do not care if the market goes up or down.

Some people think this means they do not have any market risk when, in fact, they do. The option deltas change as the price changes (see Chapter 2 - The Fundamentals Of Options for more details). This means that the position acquires a market risk as the price of the underlying instrument changes. We will highlight the ramifications of this in the decision structure below.

Please note that this strategy is particularly suited for very large investors. As will become apparent in the decision structure below, the larger the position, the better the trade will work. Ratio covered call writing is not attractive for investors who can only afford a few contracts.

EQUIVALENT STRATEGY

Ratio Covered Put Write

The ratio covered put write has virtually identical characteristics to the ratio covered call write. The choice of which to initiate will largely be a function of liquidity and order execution. In general, calls are more liquid than puts, and therefore will be easier to trade and will have a tighter bid/ask spread. On the other hand, since puts are less liquid, you may have an opportunity to get a better price if you are patient. You could enter your order at a price and hopefully someone else will enter a market order, and you will get filled a good price.

RISK/REWARD

A discussion of the risk/reward of a ratio covered call writing program is more complex than nearly all other option strategies. This is because a ratio covered call program is expected to be a *dynamic* program. The risk/reward parameters outlined below apply only to the initial position. The risk/reward characteristics change as the price of the underlying instrument and the composition of the position changes. For example, there should be no losses on a theoretically perfect ratio covered call writing program that is being dynamically managed, yet we have included discussions of risk and break-even points.

Investment

The investment will be the same as a covered call write and the sum of the margin requirements of the naked short calls. For example, if you long one underlying instrument and short two calls, you have, for margin purposes, one covered call write and one naked short call.

Break-even point

The formulas for the two break-evens for a ratio covered call write are:

Up-side break-even = strike price + (maximum profit/(number of calls written - number of underlying instruments bought))

Down-side break-even = Strike price - (maximum profit/number of underlying instruments bought)

For stocks, the number of underlying instruments is the number of round lots that were bought. If you owned 250 shares of stock, you would insert 2.5 in the formula.

Maximum risk

The maximum risk of a ratio covered call write is unlimited. You will lose a point for every point the underlying instrument rises when its price climbs above the up-side break-even. On the down-side, the risk is limited by the fact that the price of the underlying instrument cannot go below zero.

DECISION STRUCTURE

The decision structure of ratio covered call writing is like trying to hit a moving target because of the dynamic nature. The following comments will identify the major considerations when making decisions.

Selection

A ratio covered call writing program is largely a method to capture the time premium of options. This usually means that the best option to sell is the at-the-money option, because it is the option that typically has the most time premium. You will usually be writing two calls for every underlying instrument.

The problem with the at-the-money call is that it is harder to fine-tune your position when you are carrying only a small position. This will be discussed in greater detail in the sections below on follow-up strategies. The point to remember here is that you will need more out-of-the-money options to create a delta neutral position than in-the-money or at-the-money options. The additional options make it easier to adjust your position after entering the trade. This is not a problem when you are carrying a position that contains hundreds of options contracts, but does present a problem when you are carrying a small position of just a few options contracts.

A change in implied volatility will affect the price of the written call. Your preference should be to write options that have a high implied volatility when you expect declining volatility. The worst circumstance would be to write a call with low implied volatility with the expectation of increasing volatility.

If the Price of the Underlying Instrument Changes Significantly

Basically, you will be trying to keep the position as delta neutral as possible throughout the life of the trade. This will theoretically eliminate price risk as a consideration. In addition, it should maximize the amount of time premium that is captured. The tricky thing is to keep the trade delta neutral. The problem is that the deltas of the options change as the price of the underlying instrument changes. If the price of the underlying instrument climbs, the delta of the options increases, thus making you increasingly short. A declining underlying instrument will make your position increasingly long. You therefore must continually change the number of options you are short.

For example, you are long 100 contracts of the S&P 500 futures contract at 250 and short 200 contracts of the S&P 500 options with a strike of 250 and a delta of .50. If the price of the S&P 500 climbs to 260, the delta of the options will climb to, say, .55. Thus, you will be the equivalent of short 10 contracts of the futures. This can be found by taking the delta of the futures, always 1.00, times the number of futures, 100, and subtracting the number of options, 200 times the delta, .55 ((1.00 × 100) - (.55 × 200) = -10). You will now be exposed to risk if the market continues higher.

You must therefore adjust the number of contracts you are using to reduce the net delta of the position to zero. To find the new quantity of options, divide the net delta of the long side, in this example, 100 (a delta of 1.00 × the number of futures 100 = 100), by the new delta, .55. The result, 181.8, will have to be rounded to 182. You should then liquidate 18 of your short futures to bring your portfolio to the proper weighting, 182.

Note that you will have to resell those 18 contracts if the price of the underlying instrument drops back down to 250. In addition, a further drop in price would require you to sell additional contracts.

It should be clear that ratio covered call writing requires active management. You simply cannot go away for a vacation and expect to still have a delta neutral position. Note also that the more the price moves in one direction, the more the delta is moving against you.

A second adjustment should also be made to the position after the price of the underlying instrument has moved. Remember, the point of the trade is to capture time premium. Therefore, you should roll up or down as the price of the underlying instrument moves from the initial strike price to another strike price. For example, if the price of the S&P 500 futures moves from 250 to 260, you should buy back your 250 calls and sell 260 calls. Conversely, if the price of the underlying should drop to a lower strike price, you should roll down out of your current strike price and into the new at-the-money option.

There are two major problems with the ratio covered call writing program.

First, how often should the portfolio be rebalanced? Theoretically, you should rebalance every time there is a price change that implies a change of one contract in the short call position. The trade-off is that continual adjusting may create too many commissions. This will occur if the price of the underlying instrument jumps back and forth in a narrow range. You will adjust your short call portfolio with every jump in the price of the underlying instrument, creating commission expenses, yet the price won't really break out of its range.

Unfortunately, there is little that can be done about this except to not adjust the portfolio as often as would be suggested by keeping the trade delta neutral. The risk of this tactic is that the market will move enough in one direction to create a market exposure, and you will lose money because of this exposure.

In the final analysis, it is probably better to adjust whenever necessary and pay the extra commissions as the cost of not exposing yourself to market risk.

If the Option is About to Expire

You are faced with several decisions if your calls are about to expire. The time premium will have essentially vanished. There is no desirability to holding a short call if the time premium is gone. You should either liquidate the trade or roll forward. The decision is largely based on the premium levels of the next contract month. If premium levels are high, then you should consider rolling forward. If they are low, you should consider doing a ratio covered call writing program against another instrument.

WRITE AGAINST A CONVERTIBLE SECURITY

It is often more profitable to write calls against convertible securities. The most common convertible security is the convertible bond, although convertible preferreds and warrants are also candidates. A complete discussion of using convertibles is included in Chapter 7 - Covered Call Writing. That discussion assumes that only the equivalent of one call will be written. To adapt that section to ratio covered call writing, take the analysis in that section but adjust for the delta.

9

Naked Put Writing

A. Strategy
B. Equivalent strategy
C. Risk/reward
D. Decision structure

STRATEGY

Naked put writing is selling a put without owning the underlying instrument. If your portfolio consisted of only a short OEX put, you would be short a naked put.

Naked put writing is a bullish strategy. Put writers want the price of the underlying instrument to rise so they may buy back the put at a lower price. The best situation for a naked put writer is for the price of the underlying instrument to move above the put's strike price at expiration, thus rendering the put worthless. The naked put writer will have captured all of the premium as profit.

Notice that the naked put write has a limited profit potential yet unlimited loss potential. However, some studies have suggested that over 75 percent of options expire worthless.

The choice between shorting a naked put or buying the underlying instrument is based on several criteria. Let's look first at the situation at expiration. In terms of price action, the naked put is superior if the price of the underlying instrument is at the break-even point (discussed below) up to the strike price plus the put premium. Above that level, the long underlying instrument is superior. In other words, a very bullish outlook is better served by buying the underlying instrument, whereas a less bullish outlook is better served by selling the naked put.

The situation before expiration is different. If you intend to actively manage your naked puts, then selling naked puts can be as attractive as buying the underlying instrument. The use of naked put writes as a substitute for buying the underlying instrument requires active management to mitigate, though not eliminate, the additional risk. The form of active management is detailed throughout the rest of this chapter.

One disadvantage of selling a put is that you are liable for dividend or interest payments, if applicable. The payment of dividends or interest causes the put to gain an equivalent amount in value, and thus reduce the profitability.

An advantage of the naked put is that time is on the side of the naked put seller. As the option nears expiration, the time premium on the put evaporates and reduces the value of the put.

EQUIVALENT STRATEGY

An essentially equivalent strategy can be created by being long the underlying instrument and selling a call. It is unlikely that you will want to buy the instrument and sell the call if you can simply sell the put. Selling the put is easier to execute and will cost less in commissions.

The only time the equivalent strategy makes sense is if you already have one of the two legs on and want to change the character of the trade. Suppose you are very bullish and buy the underlying instrument. Later, you decide the market is not as bullish and may even slump temporarily. This is the type of situation where you may initiate a synthetic naked put write.

RISK/REWARD

Break-even Point

The break-even point at expiration is equal to the strike price minus the put premium. For example, if the strike is $50 and the put premium is $3, then the price of the underlying instrument cannot be less than $47 at the expiration of the put.

The break-even point prior to expiration is the same as the break-even point at expiration, assuming that other pricing variables, such as the implied volatility and the risk-free rate, have not changed in the meantime.

Profit Potential

The maximum profit potential is the premium received when the put is sold. This will occur only if the price of the underlying instrument is higher than the strike price at expiration. The reason that the maximum profit potential is only reached at expiration is that the option will always have time premium up to the last minutes of trading. You therefore have to let the option expire before the maximum profit potential can be reached.

The naked put will also profit at expiration if the price of the underlying instrument lies between the strike price and the strike price minus the put premium. The rule in this case is: The profit equals the put premium minus the strike price plus the price of the underlying instrument.

Before expiration, the naked put will be making money if the price of the underlying instrument has rallied since initiating the naked put write. The profit (or loss) can be estimated by the delta of the option. For example, if you sold an option for $5 with a delta of .50, then the option will be close to $3 if the price of the underlying instrument has jumped $4. Note that deltas change as the price and implied volatility change. This means that you can only estimate the future value of the option, not pinpoint it precisely.

A drop in implied volatility can increase profits. This occurs because the price of an option is largely determined by the implied volatility. A reduction in the implied volatility will reduce the value of the options, thus creating a more profitable situation for you. In fact, you can make money on a naked put if the implied volatility drops and the price of the underlying instrument stays the same. You need an options valuation model to determine the effect of the shift.

Potential Risk

The risk in holding a naked option is unlimited. As a practical matter, of course, you should be taking defensive measures before losses climb out of sight. The risk is that the price of the underlying instrument will fall while you are short the put. The dollar risk can be estimated by multiplying the option delta by the price change of the underlying instrument. For example, you will lose $3 if the delta is .30 and the price of the underlying instrument drops $10.

One risk is that the option will be assigned before you wish to exit the trade. This risk is largely controlled by your selection of strike price. An in-the-money has a chance of early exercise, while an out-of-the-money option has very little chance of early exercise.

An increase in volatility will hurt your position because it will increase the value of the option. For example, assume an at-the-money option on a $50 instrument with 90 days to expiration and implied volatility of 10 percent. This option will be worth about .98. An increase in implied volatility to 15 percent will boost the price of the option to $1.47 without any change in the price of the underlying instrument.

DECISION STRUCTURE

Selection

Market outlook is critical to the selection of the option to write. The more bullish you are the higher the strike price you will select. The reasons for this are that the delta will be higher for a higher strike price than for a lower strike, and the premium is higher, thus affording greater profit potential. A more defensive posture is to sell at lower strike prices. An out-of-the-money option has less chance of being in-the-money at expiration than an in-the-money option. The trade-off is that the premium and, hence, the profit potential, is less.

One strategy is to sell options that have a strike price lower than the implied volatility suggests as the range in the relevant time period. For example, the Swiss franc is currently trading at 61.00, the implied volatility is 12 percent, and there are 3 months left to trade the option. Implied volatility suggests that prices will trade in a range of 1.83 (3 percent times 61.00) above and below 61.00. This suggests selecting a put 1.83 lower than the current market price, perhaps the 59.00 call. A more conservative approach would be to sell a put even lower, perhaps twice the range suggested by the implied volatility.

Implied volatility has a major impact on the selection of the underlying instrument to write a put against. The best strategy is to sell options that have a high implied volatility, while looking for prices to rise and volatility to fall. It is very helpful to keep a record or graph of the implied volatilities for the recent past. This will provide a perspective on the volatility of the put you want to write. In general, you will want to write puts that have a high implied volatility rather than a low implied volatility.

Selling a put is a way of selling time premium. Selling puts is most attractive, all other things being equal, when there is little time left before expiration. Time decay is limited in the first days after an option is listed. As time progresses, the time decay accelerates, making selling options more attractive the closer expiration approaches.

If the Price of the Underlying Instrument Rises

If you are no longer bullish, simply liquidate the trade and take your profits.

If you are still bullish, you have three possibilities. First, continue holding your existing position. This can be very attractive if the put is out-of-the-money and there is little time left before expiration. This strategy also suits a market stance that is only slightly bullish.

A more bullish market stance suggests rolling up to a higher strike price. This will give you more profit potential, because the delta and the premium will be higher.

If the option is about to expire, you can roll forward. The selection of which option to roll forward into will be related to your market outlook. You probably don't want to liquidate your existing put if the time premium is falling rapidly and there is little chance for the option to go in-the-money. In this circumstance, you may want to take a larger risk and sell options on the next expiration while still holding the nearby options. The reward is that you capture the time premium on the nearby contract, while holding your longer term position in the farther contract. The risk is that the market will plunge sharply and you will lose money on both the nearby and the farther options simultaneously.

If the Price of the Underlying Instrument Drops

If the market is moving against you and you look for it to continue to move against you, liquidation of the position makes the most sense.

Another plan, if you have turned bearish, is to sell the underlying instrument (if it is possible to short the underlying instrument). You will have converted the short put into a covered put write. The critical question is whether to sell the underlying instrument in the same quantity as the short put, or in a delta neutral quantity. Using the same quantity is more bearish than placing positions in a delta neutral quantity. (See Chapter 10 - Covered Put Writing and Chapter 11 - Ratio Covered Put Writing for more details.)

If you think the slump is temporary, you could continue to hold your current position or roll down. Holding the current position is more aggressive than rolling down. The higher strike will have more risk and reward than the lower strike.

If the option is about to expire and you are still bullish, you can roll forward. The selection of which strike to sell will follow the guidelines outlined above. One decision you will need to make is whether to liquidate the current position and the attendant sharp decay in time premium or to sell the far options and hang onto the current position. The question comes down to your market outlook. Will the price drop more than the time decay? If so, then roll forward. If not, hang onto the current position and sell the next expiration option.

10

Covered Put Writing

A. Strategy
B. Equivalent strategy
C. Risk/reward
D. Decision structure
E. Diversification of profit and protection

STRATEGY

Covered put writing is being short an underlying instrument and short a put on that instrument.

The table below shows the various puts available and the instruments that the put could be written against:

Stock indexes

Short futures contract

Futures

Cash instrument/commodity
Futures contract
Put with higher strike price and same expiration

Theoretically, you could do a covered put writing program on stocks. However, it is harder to short stocks, particularly listed stocks, and so there tend to be few covered put writing programs on stocks.

The quantity represented by the number of puts sold is equal to the quantity of the underlying instrument. For example, covered put writing using options on gold will have one short put option for every short contract. (Ratio put writing is the strategy of using differing quantities of the underlying instrument and put options, and is outlined in Chapter 11 - Ratio Covered Put Writing.)

There are three main reasons behind covered put writing:

1. Partially hedge existing position against price increases.
2. Increase return on existing short position.
3. Furnish opportunity for profit.

EQUIVALENT STRATEGY

Naked Call Write

The naked call write can be substituted in many cases for a covered put write, particularly with instruments that pay dividends or interest. There are several main considerations for deciding whether to naked call write or covered put write. The first is the commission structure. Commissions will be significantly higher for covered put writes than for naked call writes. The second consideration is the total return from the investment. A covered put write on stocks or debt instruments is responsible for dividend or interest payments that can cut the return even further. The third consideration is that you may already be short the underlying instrument so that covered writing may be the only practical action. The alternative would be to buy back the underlying instrument and initiate a naked call write. It may be cheaper in commissions to simply sell the puts against the instrument than liquidate and start a new position from scratch.

A major difference between a naked call write and a covered put write is that the covered put write provides a measure of up-side protection but a naked call write does not. A naked call write is thus a more aggressive position.

RISK/REWARD

Maximum Profit Potential

The maximum profit potential is equal to the underlying instrument price minus the strike price of the option plus the price of the put.

Maximum profit potential = UI price - strike price + put price

Let's look at an example of the maximum profit potential. You sell short one contract of Treasury-bond futures at 90.00 with the strike price of the option at 91.00 and the option premium at 2.00. Your maximum profit potential is 90.00 minus 91.00 plus 2.00, or 1.00.

Break-even Point and Down-side Protection

Covered put writing partially hedges both up and down price moves. Figure 10.1 shows the profit/loss diagram for a covered put at expiration. The short put limits the profit potential of the short underlying instrument, but buffers the short position from losses by the amount of the premium only.

Losses may be reduced but not limited. Losses are reduced because you receive the put premium, which buffers you from the full value of a price increase. Covered puts show significant losses as the instrument rallies above the break-even point. The maximum theoretical risk is unlimited because the price of the underlying instrument has no theoretical cap.

On the other hand, covered put writing has limited profit potential. Figure 10.1 shows how the total profit is limited when the instrument price falls below the maximum gain level. At that point, gains in the underlying instrument are matched dollar for dollar with the losses in the short put at expiration.

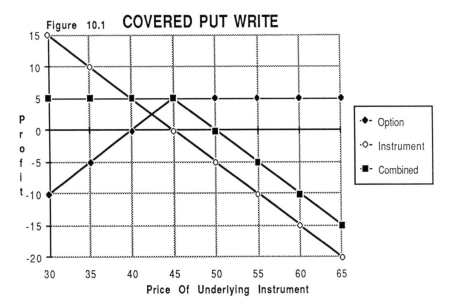

Figure 10.1 **COVERED PUT WRITE**

The break-even point shows the amount of up-side protection that the covered put position provides. One advantage of covered put writing is that it is possible to increase the break-even point to above the initial entry level.

The break-even point, in formula form, is:

Break-even point = underlying price + put premium

For example, use the assumptions of a Treasury-bond futures price of 90.00, a strike price of 91.00, and a put premium of 2.00. The futures price (90.00) plus the put premium (2.00) equals the break-even point (92.00).

Figure 10.2 shows the break-even point for this example. Note that you sold the futures at 90.00 but you will not lose money unless it is above 92.00 at the expiration of the option. For example, suppose the futures contract is at 91.00 at expiration. This means that the put options will be worth zero but you will have the 2.00 that you received when you sold the option for a net profit on the option of

2.00. However, you will have a loss on the futures contract of 1.00, the difference between the current value of the futures contract and the selling price. This net is that you have a 2 point profit from the sale of the option, minus the 1 point loss on the purchase of the bond futures, for a total profit of 1 point.

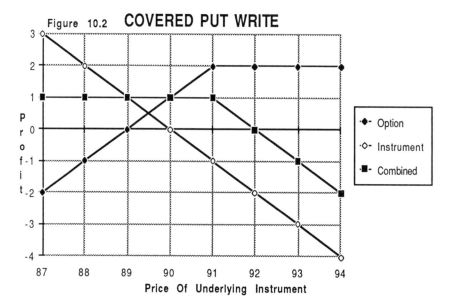

Figure 10.2 **COVERED PUT WRITE**

You can lose money before the expiration of the contract if the price of the underlying instrument increases. For example, suppose the bond futures went to 92.00 the first day after initiating a covered put position. The value of the put will have dropped below its initial 2.00 price but not enough to offset the loss in the futures contract, because the delta is less than 1.00. This occurs because the value of the put is composed mainly of time value rather than intrinsic value. The decline will be greater if the option is in the money because it will have more intrinsic value. Remember that the break-even point describes the situation only at the expiration of the option.

The break-even point outlined above describes the situation at expiration only. Before then, the break-even point changes with time. The break-even point on the first day in the trade is the entry level. Over time, the break-even point will move above the entry level. The time value of the put decays, creating the profits that raise the break-even point. This shows that a covered put program can stack the odds in your favor.

The up-side protection, specified by the break-even point, is affected by the strike price of the put. A covered put using a higher strike price write will have greater up-side protection than using a lower strike price. The greater premium income provides greater up-side protection.

Net Investment Required

The investment required depends on the instrument. For stocks, you will need the collateral to carry a short position, but will receive the option premium.

The investment for a covered write in futures is the premium of the option (marked to the market) plus the greater of the underlying futures margin minus one-half of the amount that the option is in-the-money, or one-half the amount of the underlying futures margin.

One facet to remember is that being short stock means that you are liable for dividends, and that your investment will increase if you are holding the position during a dividend payment. The same is true for being short cash bonds. Your investment will increase if there is a coupon payment.

The Investment Return

There are two major ways to calculate the return on your investment. Each one presents a different perspective on the proposed trade. Both should be examined before initiating a position.

Return if Exercised

The return if exercised is the return on the investment if the short underlying instrument is called away. The return to exercise depends on the type of option and the price action after trade entry. An out-of-the-money option must have the underlying instrument drop in price to below the strike price or there is no return if exercised. This is because the option will not be exercised if it is out-of-the-money, and thus no return if exercised. An in-the-money covered write only requires the instrument price to remain unchanged. You will receive the return if exercised for an in-the-money covered write even if the instrument price is unchanged. The return if exercised is the same as the return if unchanged for an in-the-money write (see Return if Unchanged, below). Remember that the deeper the option is in-the-money, the higher the probability that the return if exercised will actually be attained. Comparing the relative merits of different strike prices used in covered writes requires an assumption about the direction of prices.

Let's look at an example, an out-of-the-money covered write. Assume you are selling an April 65 Widget put at $4, against your short futures position initiated at $68. Assume that the net investment is $2400, and that each $1 move in the futures contract is worth $100. If the option is exercised, you will make $3 on the short sale of the futures (68 - 65 = 3), plus $4 on the sale of the put. The total return will be $7, worth $700, on the investment of $2400.

The return if exercised in this example is 29 percent (700/2400 = 29 percent). You should also look at the annualized return for better comparison with other investments. Suppose you held the Widget covered put position for three months. Your annualized return would be 117 percent (29 percent return for 3 months is equivalent to 117 percent return for 1 year).

Return if Unchanged

The return if unchanged is the return on your investment if there is no change in the price of the underlying instrument from the date of entry to expiration. This method of calculating return has a major advantage over the return if exercised; it makes no assumption about future prices. It gives a closer approximation of the return you should expect. The return if unchanged is the same as the return if exercised for an in-the-money write (see Return if Exercised, above).

DECISION STRUCTURE

The decision structure for a covered put program has the usual selection and two follow-up strategies. However, the selection of a covered put is dependent on the rationale behind the trade. Each reason has a unique selection structure. There is one factor that affects all three strategies.

A change in implied volatility will affect the price of the written put. Your preference should be to write options that have a high implied volatility, if you expect declining volatility. The worst circumstance would be to write a put with low implied volatility with the expectation of increasing volatility.

What Is Your Strategy?

Now, let's look at the three main reasons behind covered put writing:

1. Partially hedge existing position against price decline.
2. Increase return on existing long position.
3. Furnish opportunity for profit.

Hedge Existing Position

The first strategy is to write a put against an instrument you think is going to rise in price near term but will move higher long term. The idea is that the option premium will protect you against the price rise without having to post any additional funds. In addition, you may make a little money on the decay of the time value. However, remember that selling a put may mean that you will have to give up your short position if the put is exercised. You may have protected a position you will no longer have. In fact, the short put will protect the instrument price against a small price rise, but the strategy falls apart if the market drops. You will have your instrument called away if the put is exercised. You wanted to carry the instrument until a particular time but the market took it away early. To partially protect against this, use an option that doesn't expire until after you want to liquidate the short put. Look at other hedge strategies, such as buying calls (see Chapter 4 - Buy A Call).

This strategy implies the sale of an in-the-money put to provide protection. Select the quantity of the in-the-money put that has a delta that will cover the expected price rise. Remember, very in-the-money puts often have poor liquidity, and entering and exiting the short put may be difficult.

Be sure to have the proper number of short options. Find the option's delta to construct a delta neutral position to make sure you have enough puts to provide adequate protection.

Increase Return

The second strategy is to increase return on an existing position. Where do you think the price of the underlying instrument is going? If you are long-term bullish, get out of the instrument and invest in something else. If you are bearish, treat the covered put write as a separate trade and follow the decision outlined in the section below. When you write a put against an existing position, you are no longer in that existing position. Many investors psychologically cling to the short position and do not realize that the sale of the put means that they have liquidated a short position and simultaneously initiated a covered put write. These are two separate trades with differing risk/reward characteristics and decision structures.

Selling a put is a powerful way to increase returns on an instrument for which you have a predetermined buy point. Selling a put at the strike price that corresponds to the buy point increases your returns by the amount of the premium, while reducing the risk. Selling a put is essentially prebuying your short instrument. When the instrument rises to your target price, the put buyer may call away your instrument. The critical problem is identifying a valid target purchase price.

It is a problem when you have an objective that is below the lowest strike price, or when the premium for the strike price at your target is very low. A premium worth only $50 is not high enough to sell. It is probably a better strategy in this case to sell a strike price close to the current instrument price and continually roll down by selling additional puts as the instrument price drops to your objective. The selling of additional puts essentially changes this from a covered put to a ratio covered put. It is essential that you roll down for a credit; otherwise you are not increasing your returns.

Furnish Opportunity for Profit

First determine your market attitude. A stable market outlook is the best time to sell puts if premiums are high. If you are bullish on the underlying instrument, don't write puts. If you are very bearish on the underlying instrument, sell out-of-the-money puts (or wait until later to sell the put). This will give you the greatest profit potential, though you will give up some up-side protection. An alternative strategy for the very bearish is to not sell as many options as underlying instruments. For example, sell 3 puts against your short 400 shares of United Widget. If risk protection is more important, sell in-the-money puts. You will be cutting your potential return, but you won't have as great a risk of loss as selling out-of-the-money puts. Be careful that you are not cutting your potential return to such a low level that it doesn't compensate for the risk. Your subjective criterion of risk versus profit potential, combined with the range of available in-the-money and out-of-the-money options, allows you to fine-tune your covered put program.

There are at least three statistics you need to consider when covered put writing: break-even point, return if exercised, and return if unchanged. Annualize the return figures to make them easier to compare with each other and with other covered writes. Comparing annualized returns is useful, but those yields are not engraved in stone. You must evaluate the probability of those returns being achieved. You may find one covered put with an annualized return if unchanged of 40 percent, and another one of only 20 percent. The second covered write is a better investment if your estimation of the chance of success for the first one is only 30 percent, while the chance for the second write is 80 percent.

Another consideration is the down-side protection of the proposed trade. You need to find the right combination of profit potential with risk protection. Filter the universe of potential writes to those that provide the minimum amount of desired protection.

If the Price of the Underlying Instrument Rises

There are two choices. The first is to liquidate the trade. This is preferred choice if you are now very bullish and think the price of the underlying instrument will never move back below your break-even point.

The second choice, rolling up, can provide additional protection while keeping the possibility of profit should the market move higher. It is called rolling up because as the price of the underlying instrument moves higher you buy back the original put and sell a put with a higher strike price. The additional premium provides additional up-side protection, though profit potential becomes more limited. If the price of the underlying instrument continues up and you keep selling puts, you may be locking in a loss. The question then becomes: Is the loss from rolling up bigger than the loss of letting my current position ride? Remember, you are, in effect, initiating a new position, so the criteria for entering a new position apply.

For example, you are short widget futures at $190 and short a June 200 put at $18. Your up-side protection extends up to $208 (excluding transaction and carrying costs). Two weeks later the government releases its widget crop report that shows large plantings of widgets. The price of widgets rises to $208, while the June 180 put drops to $2 and the 200 call is trading for $15. You've lost two points on your position and have reached the break-even point. The price of widgets will have to be unchanged to split even. You have little protection left in your June 180 put, but you can increase protection by selling the June 200 put and buying back the June 180 put.

After this transaction, you have down-side protection to $221 because you sold a net premium of $13 (the price of the June 200 put, $15, minus the price of the June 180 put, $2). The premium collected is added to the original break-even point to derive the new break-even point. You will make 13 points at the current level if the widget price is unchanged. Rolling up gained additional protection and a chance to make money at the higher level. If you stuck with the original position, you would have made only the 2 points remaining on the June 180 put.

The problem with rolling up is that you are reducing your profit potential. You have agreed to have your widget future called away at $200 rather than at $180. You have, in effect, swapped additional protection for reduced profit protection.

The key is when, if ever, to roll down. This is a market timing decision. Liquidate the trade if you have turned bullish. If you are still bearish, the point to roll up might be at the original break-even point, at a technical resistance point, or at a money management point.

The real problem arises when the price rises quickly, you don't respond quickly enough, and the market presents you with only an opportunity to roll up and lock in a loss. This is more likely with out-of-the-money writes because they provide less up-side protection. The choice may simply be to lock in a small loss rather than carry the risk of a much larger loss. Be alert to negative price moves and have a plan for rolling up firmly in place before initiating the original write.

There are three other ways to roll up. First, roll up part of your position and keep part in the original call. This increases your up-side protection but gives higher profit potential than rolling up the entire position.

The second way to roll up is to keep the original write, and write another put at the higher strike price. This becomes, in effect, a ratio write with two strike prices. You will be short two puts against one short underlying instrument. Take a look at Chapter 11 - Ratio Covered Put Writing for more details on the strategic implications and the risk/reward characteristics.

The third way is to roll up and forward. In other words, buy back your original put and sell a put at a higher strike price in the next expiration month. This has the advantage/disadvantage of giving more time for your trade to work or backfire. One possibility is to partially roll up and forward. Keep some of your original write and roll up and forward some into the next expiration month. Note that rolling up and forward restricts the maximum profit potential for a longer period of time.

If the Price of the Underlying Instrument Drops

The first choice is to liquidate the trade and take the profit you had planned. This is particularly attractive if the return comes quickly. There are two other possibilities: letting the instrument get called away and rolling down.

The instrument will likely be called away from you if its price drops below the strike price. This is simply another way of liquidating the trade. When the put is exercised, you will have disposed of the put and the underlying instrument at the same time (unless you decide to hold the short underlying instrument and short another underlying instrument to deliver). You will receive the return if exercised on the trade.

In many cases, it is better to roll forward rather that have the underlying instrument called away. You will be saving commissions and, as was pointed out above, this can increase the return significantly. You will certainly want to roll forward if there is not much time premium left and you are still bearish or neutral.

Another alternative is to roll down. This means writing more puts at higher strike prices as the price of the underlying instrument drops, while buying back the original short put. The key is market timing. You should keep writing puts as the market moves lower, but not to the point where the price begins to rise.

Rolling down increases the maximum profit potential at the expense of the break-even point. Whereas rolling up is a credit transaction and you receive cash, rolling down is a debit transaction. You must pay additional cash. The break-even point is raised by the amount of the debit. However, you could combine the rolling down with rolling forward to the next expiration month as a potential tactic to reduce the debit.

If the Option is About to Expire

You are faced with several decisions if your puts are about to expire. The time premium will have essentially vanished. There is no desirability to holding a short put if the time premium is gone. You should either liquidate the trade or roll forward and/or down. The decision is largely based on your market expectation. If your covered put position is profitable, you need to ask if your attitude on the market is bullish or bearish. If you are bearish, roll forward into the next expiring option month if the premium levels are attractive. You are, in effect, initiating a new position, so the criteria for entering a new position apply. For example, you need to decide if an in-the-money or out-of-the-money put is appropriate.

A criterion for determining if you should roll forward is the return per day. However, it is only applicable for rolling forward into the same strike price. For example, you may be able to make $435 for the 23 days left on your current write, but $1919 on a write on the next expiration month that expires in 83 days. Your return-per-day on the current write is $18.91 (435/23 = 18.91), while the write on the next expiration month returns $23.12 (1919/83 = 23.12).

You should probably liquidate the trade if you are bullish. It is rarely wise to carry a covered put when you are bullish unless you are expecting a slight and temporary rally in the market. You can always write another put on the next expiration cycle when the rally is over.

If the option is about to expire and your total position is unprofitable, you have a couple of alternatives. Liquidate the trade unless you see an imminent market turnaround. If you are still bearish, you could roll forward and up.

DIVERSIFICATION OF PROFIT AND PROTECTION

The goal of your covered put writing is to find covered puts that provide the right combination of profit potential and risk protection. The problem is that the maximum profit potential comes from writing out-of-the-money puts, while the best protection comes from writing in-the-money puts. Another problem with writing only one type of option is that you are committed to just one strategy, and the potential for the strategy to fail is relatively high. However, you can diversify your portfolio of covered puts by using multiple strike prices. A combination of in-the-money and out-of-the-money options may provide a better balance of profit potential and risk protection. There will be a greater chance of achieving the expected results because you have diversified the potential risks and rewards across a broader array of strike prices.

Another way to increase the chances of achieving your expected return is to diversify through time. You can write puts at the same strike price in different expiration months. For example, you could write the April and July Amalgamated Widget 85 puts.

Combining these two techniques adds another dimension to your strategy. You can fine-tune the write program according to your expectations of future prices. For example, you may think that Widget and Associates will be $25 by April and $15 by July. You could write two out-of-the-money puts: an April 25 and a July 15. Alternately, you could write an in-the-money put at the nearest expiration to provide protection now, but write an out-of-the-money put in the next expiration month to provide greater profit potential.

11

Ratio Covered
Put Writing

A. Strategy
B. Equivalent strategy
C. Risk/reward
D. Decision structure

STRATEGY

Ratio covered put writing is being short an underlying instrument, and short more puts on that instrument than you have of that instrument. For instance, you could be short one S&P 500 futures contract and short two puts.

The main rationale for a ratio covered put write is to capture the time premium of the short puts. This is accomplished by buying the underlying instrument and selling enough puts to create a delta neutral position. This means that the sum of the deltas of the short puts will be equal to the delta of the short underlying instrument. For instance, you sell one S&P 500 futures contract at 225 and sell 2 225 put options with deltas of .50 each. The delta on the short stock index futures is 1.00, so you need to sell options that have a total delta of 1.00. In this case, you needed to sell two puts because their deltas were .50.

Note that you have initiated a position that has a delta of zero. This means that you have no market exposure. This shows that a delta neutral ratio covered put write is a neutral strategy. You do not care if the market goes up or down.

Some people think this means that they do not have any market risk when, in fact, they do. The option deltas change as the price changes (see Chapter 2 - The Fundamentals Of Options for more details). This means that the position acquires a market risk as the price of the underlying changes. We'll highlight the ramifications of this in the decision structure below.

Please note that this strategy is particularly suited for very large investors. As will become apparent in the decision structure below, the larger the position, the better the trade will work. Ratio covered put writing is not attractive for investors who can only afford a few contracts.

EQUIVALENT STRATEGY

Ratio Covered Call Write

The ratio covered call write has virtually identical characteristics to the ratio covered put write. The choice of which to initiate will largely be a function of liquidity and order execution. In general, calls are more liquid than puts, and therefore will be easier to trade and have a tighter bid/ask spread. On the other hand, the lesser liquidity of the puts may give you an opportunity to get a better price if you are patient. You could enter your order at a price, and hopefully someone else will enter a market order, and you can get filled at a good price.

Covered call writing is virtually always a superior strategy over covered put writing when the underlying instrument pays dividends or interest payments. The covered put writer is liable for the dividend or interest payments. This increases the cost without increasing the return. Covered put writing on instruments such as futures contracts does not have the same drawback.

RISK/REWARD

The risk/reward of a ratio covered put writing program is more complex than nearly all other option strategies, because it is expected to be a *dynamic* program. The risk/reward parameters outlined below apply only to the initial position, and change as the price of the underlying instrument and the composition of the position changes. For example, there should be no losses on a theoretically perfect ratio covered put writing program that is being dynamically managed. In addition, the risk/reward characteristics are the same as for a ratio covered call write program. The only major difference is in the investment.

The investment will be the same as a covered put write and the sum of the margin requirements of the naked short puts. For example, if you short one underlying instrument and two puts, you have, for margin purposes, one covered put write and one naked short put.

DECISION STRUCTURE

The decision structure of ratio covered put writing is like trying to hit a moving target, because of its dynamic nature. The following comments identify the major considerations when making decisions.

Selection

A ratio covered put writing program is largely a method to capture the time premium of options. This usually means that the best option to sell is the at-the-money option because it typically has the most time premium. You will usually be writing two puts for every underlying instrument.

The problem with the at-the-money put is that it is harder to fine-tune your position when you are carrying only a small position. This will be discussed in greater detail in the sections below on follow-up strategies. The point to remember is that you will need more out-of-the-money options to create a delta neutral position than in-the-money or at-the-money options. The additional options make it easier to adjust your position after entering the trade. This is not a problem when you are carrying hundreds of options contracts, but it does present a problem when you are carrying a small position of just a few options contracts.

A change in implied volatility will affect the price of the written put. Your preference should be to write options that have a high implied volatility with you expecting declining volatility. The worst circumstance would be to write a put with low implied volatility with the expectation of increasing volatility.

If the Price of the Underlying Instrument Changes Significantly

Try to keep the position as delta neutral as possible throughout the life of the trade. This will theoretically eliminate price risk as a consideration. In addition, it should maximize the amount of time premium that is captured. The trick is to keep the trade delta neutral. The problem is that the deltas of the options change as the price of the underlying instrument changes. If the price of the underlying instrument climbs, the delta of the options increases, thus making you increasingly short. A declining underlying instrument will make your position increasingly long. You therefore must continually change the number of options you are short.

For example, you are short 100 contracts of the S&P 500 futures contract at 250, and short 200 contracts of the S&P 500 put options with a strike of 250 and a delta of .50. If the price of the S&P 500 drops to 240, the delta of the options will climb to, say, .55. Thus, you will be the equivalent of long 10 contracts of the futures. This can be found by multiplying the number of options, 200, by the delta, .55, and subtracting the delta of the futures, always 1.00, times the number of futures, 100: $((.55 \times 200) - (1.00 \times 100) = +10)$. You will now be exposed to risk if the market continues lower.

You must therefore adjust the number of contracts you are using to reduce the net delta of the position to zero. To find the new quantity of options, divide the net delta of the long side, in this example, 100 (a delta of 1.00 $\times$ the number of futures 100 = 100), by the new delta, .55. The result, 181.8, will have to be rounded to 182. You should then liquidate 18 of your short options to bring your portfolio to the proper weighting, 182.

Note that you will have to buy back those 18 contracts if the price of the underlying instrument moves back up to 250. In addition, a further drop in price would require you to buy additional contracts.

It should be clear that ratio covered put writing requires active management. You simply cannot go away for a vacation and expect to still have a delta neutral position. Note also that the more the prices move in one direction, the more the delta is moving against you.

A second adjustment should also be made to the position after the price of the underlying instrument has moved. Remember, the point of the trade is to capture time premium. Therefore, you should roll up or down as the price of the underlying instrument moves from the initial strike price to another strike price. For example, if the price of the S&P 500 futures moves from 250 to 260, you should buy back your 250 puts and sell 260 puts. Conversely, if the price of the underlying instrument should drop to a lower strike price, you should roll down out of your current strike price and into the new at-the-money option.

There are two major problems with the ratio covered put writing program.

First, how often should the portfolio be rebalanced? Theoretically, you should rebalance every time there is a price change that implies a change of one contract in the short put position. The trade-off is that continual adjusting may create too many commissions. This will occur if the price of the underlying instrument jumps back and forth in a narrow range. You will be adjusting your short put portfolio with every drop in the price of the underlying, creating commission expense, yet the price of the underlying instrument won't really break out of its range.

Unfortunately, there is little that can be done about this except to not adjust the portfolio as often as would be suggested by keeping the trade delta neutral. The risk of this tactic is that the market moves enough in one direction to create a market exposure, and you lose money because of this exposure.

In the final analysis, it is probably better to adjust whenever necessary and pay the extra commissions as the cost of not exposing yourself to market risk.

If the Option is About to Expire

You are faced with several decisions if your puts are about to expire. The time premium will have essentially vanished. There is no desirability to holding a short put if the time premium is gone. You should either liquidate the trade or roll forward. The decision is largely based on the premium levels of the next contract month. If premium levels are high then you should consider rolling forward. If they are low, you should consider doing a ratio covered put writing program against another instrument.

12

Bull Spreads

A. Strategy
B. Risk/reward
C. Decision structure

STRATEGY

A bull spread is a bullish strategy with both limited risk and profit potential. It is not as bullish as buying a call or selling a put, but the risk is generally lower than buying a call and is significantly lower than selling a put.

A bull spread is either:

> Long a low strike call and short a high strike call, or
> Long a low strike put and short a high strike put

This is a popular spread because it usually has a low investment, has limited risk, and compares favorably with other bull strategies. Many investors will take the money they would have invested in long calls and buy bull spreads instead. In many cases, they will end up with greater profit potential than buying calls if the market moves only moderately higher.

Note the caveat of being only moderately bullish. This points up the fact that bull spreads are a strategy if you are moderately bullish, but not if you are very bullish. This is because bull spreads have limited up-side potential. You limit your up-side potential when you buy a bull spread.

Another use of the bull spread is to enhance the profitability of a long call or put. This concept requires that you are already in a long call or put position.

In any long option trade, you may find yourself in either a profitable or unprofitable situation. If you are holding a profitable long position, you can write a higher strike option to create a bull spread and help protect your profits. In effect, you have limited your profit potential, but you have also limited your risk.

Note that this strategy works for both puts and calls. However, you are bullish on the market if you are in a profitable call position but bearish if you are in a profitable put position. This means that your market attitude must turn 180 degrees if you are to use this technique for puts. For calls, this strategy is a signal that you are less bullish than before you switched to a bull spread.

RISK/REWARD

Net Investment Required

The net investment is the price of the option with the lower strike price minus the price of the call with the higher strike price.

Note that this will always be a debit transaction for a bull call spread because the lower strike call must always be priced lower than the higher strike call. Note also that it will always be a credit transaction for bull put spreads because the higher strike puts must always be priced higher than the lower strike puts.

Let's look at an example. The Major Market Index (MMI) closes at 350.30, the November 345 call is priced at 10 3/4, and the November 350 call is priced at 7 7/8. Your net investment will be a debit of the difference between the costs of the two options. In this case, you will pay 10 3/4 minus 7 7/8, or 2 7/8.

At the same time, the November 345 put was trading at 7 and the November 350 was trading at 9 1/8. Here, the trade would be initiated at a net credit of 2 1/8.

Maximum Return

The maximum return is limited for a bull spread. You will receive the maximum return if the underlying instrument is trading above the higher of the two strike prices when the options expire.

The maximum profit potential for a bull call spread is equal to the higher strike price minus the lower strike price minus the net investment. The maximum profit potential for a bull put spread is the net credit received when the trade is initiated.

Assume you initiated the bull put spread of buying the November 345 put at 7 and selling the November 350 put at 9 1/8 when the Major Market Index was trading at 350.50. You will receive the maximum profit of 2 1/8 if the MMI is still above the higher of the two strike prices, in this case, 350. Table 12.1 shows the profit and loss for each of the two options and the net profit or loss for the total position at different prices of the MMI when it expires.

Table 12.1. Bull put spread results

Price	345 put	350 put	Total profit/loss
330	+8	-10 7/8	-2 7/8
335	+3	-5 7/8	-2 7/8
340	-2	-7/8	-2 7/8
345	-7	+4 1/8	-2 7/8
347 7/8	-7	+7	0
350	-7	+9 1/8	+2 1/8
355	-7	+9 1/8	+2 1/8

Let's add another column to this chart so you can see the difference between this strategy and the outright purchase of a call. In this case, let's assume you bought the November 350 call at 7 7/8. This table shows that the purchase of the bull spread is superior to the purchase of a call, unless the market climbs significantly. The difference is particularly sharp when viewed on an equal dollar-invested basis. In this example, you could initiate about three bull spreads for the same investment as one call.

Table 12.2. Bull put spread versus call purchase

Price	345 put	350 put	Total profit/loss	Call results
330	+8	-10 7/8	-2 7/8	-7 7/8
335	+3	-5 7/8	-2 7/8	-7 7/8
340	-2	-7/8	-2 7/8	-7 7/8
345	-7	+4 1/8	-2 7/8	-7 7/8
347 7/8	-7	+7	0	-7 7/8
350	-7	+9 1/8	+2 1/8	-7 7/8
355	-7	+9 1/8	+2 1/8	-2 7/8

Maximum Risk

The maximum risk is different for bull call and bull put spreads. For bull call spreads, the maximum risk will occur when the price of the underlying instrument falls below the lower strike price. For a bull put spread, the maximum risk will occur at the point found by taking the difference in strike prices minus the net credit received.

Table 12.1 shows an example of the maximum risk and where it occurs. Table 12.3 shows the same situation for a bull call spread with the 345 call purchased for 10 3/4 and the 350 call purchased for 7 7/8.

Table 12.3. Bull call spread results

Price	345 call	350call	Total profit/loss
340	-10 3/4	+7 7/8	-2 7/8
345	-10 3/4	+7 7/8	-2 7/8
347 7/8	-7 7/8	+7 7/8	0
350	-5 3/4	+7 7/8	+2 1/8
355	-3/4	+2 7/8	+2 1/8

The dollar risk for a bull call spread is the net debit paid to initiate the position. The risk for a bull put spread is the difference between the two strike prices minus the net credit received when the trade was initiated.

The tables above show examples of these calculations, but let's show another two examples here. Assume you buy a Boeing November 55 call at 2 and sell a November 60 call at 3/8 when the stock is trading at 55. The maximum risk for this trade is the net debit of 1 5/8 (2 - 3/8 = 1 5/8). Let's look at a bull put spread where you buy the Boeing November 55 put at 1 5/8 and sell the November 60 put at 5 1/2 for a net credit of 3 7/8. Your risk is 1 1/8 (60 - 55 - 3 7/8).

Break-even Point

The break-even points for bull call and bull put spreads are slightly different. For bull put spreads, the break-even point is the high strike price minus net credit received. For bull call spreads, it is the low strike price plus net debit paid. The tables above give examples of the break-even points.

DECISION STRUCTURE

We mentioned under Strategy above that there are two possible uses for the bull spread concept: as a trade and as a profit enhancement tool. Both strategies use the same selection and follow-up strategies.

Selection

Bull spreads can be structured to reflect how bullish you are. You can make them as bullish as your market outlook. The most bullish call spread has both legs out-of-the-money, while the least bullish put spread has both legs out-of-the-money.

One critical question is whether to select the bull put or the bull call spread. In general, the risk and reward of the two different styles are very close, though some believe that put spreads tend to be slightly more attractive. For example, the ratio of the maximum profit potential to the dollar risk will tend to be slightly higher for bull put spreads than for bull call spreads. In addition, bull put spreads are credit transactions.

These advantages don't come free. One disadvantage with put spreads is that they are liable for early exercise if you are short an in-the-money option. Note that the more bullish you are, the more chance of early exercise. Thus, you may be exercised before having a chance to make the maximum profit. Another problem is that puts tend to be less liquid than calls. As a result, the bid/ask spread may be larger, and you may have more trouble entering or exiting your trade in the quantity you want.

Another negative feature of bull call spreads is that time decay is working against the bull put spreader. Time is usually working in favor of the bull call spreader due to the usually greater decline in time premium of the short call than the long call. However, time is working against the bull put spread because the long put's time premium is likely to be decaying faster than the short put's time premium.

Another consideration in selecting a bull spread is commissions, which tend to be a larger percentage of the potential profit than with other option strategies. Be sure to consider the cost of commissions before selecting a bull spread over other bullish strategies, and before selecting the strike price.

Bull spreads can be selected by looking at their maximum risk/reward weighted by the chances of occurring, based on the implied volatility or your expected volatility. The first step in this procedure is to list the ratio of maximum profit potential versus the maximum dollar risk of all possible bull spreads. Step two is to weight the results by the chance of occuring as determined by either the implied volatility or by your expected volatility. This will give you an expected return on all the bull spreads for that instrument. Unfortunately, this is a technique that essentially requires a computer to go through the myriad of computations.

If the Price of the Underlying Instrument Drops

If you still expect prices to move higher, you could:

> Hold the existing position
> Liquidate the short call option if in a bull call spread
> Liquidate the long put option if in a bull put spread
> Roll down

Holding the existing position is the most common tactic. No further computations of break-evens and risks and rewards are necessary. You know what your risk is and, in fact, you may already have moved to below the point of maximum risk. If this is the case, you have nothing further to lose on this trade.

A more aggressive tactic is to liquidate the short call option if you are in a bull call spread or liquidate the long put option if you are in a bull put spread. This changes the character of the trade to either a long call or a short put. The net effect is that you have thrown in the towel on the bull spread and are now taking a more bullish stance on the market. Your rationale may be that the market was only somewhat bullish at higher levels, but is much more bullish at these lower levels. The problem with this tactic is that it is too easy to rationalize and emotionally make a decision in an effort to "double up and catch up." Many traders, when confronted with a losing position, will take on too much risk in an effort to recapture their losses. The net effect is that there is nothing intrinsically wrong with this tactic, but it must be done rationally. Let's look at the bull call spread used in Table 12.3 as an example.

Assume the market dipped to 340 the day after you entered the bull spread. The 345 call is now selling for 2 3/4 and the 350 is selling at 1. Your choice is to stick with the bull call spread or to liquidate the short 350 call. Table 12.4 shows the results at different price levels of these two strategies. Remember that shifting to a long call at this point means that you are starting out with a loss of 2 7/8. This loss is counted in the results of the long call. Notice that prices must move significantly higher before you will make a profit on the long call.

Table 12.4. Bull call spread and long call results

Price	Bull spread	Long call
335	-2 7/8	-5 5/8
340	-2 7/8	-5 5/8
345	-2 7/8	-5 5/8
347 7/8	0	-2 3/4
350	+2 1/8	-5/8
355	+2 1/8	+4 3/8

The alternative is to liquidate the long put. The problem with this is that you have shifted to a position that probably has little time premium in it, and the profits will not be large enough to cover the loss on the original spread. You will therefore rarely want to liquidate the long put if you are in bull put spread, but selling the short call can be a very viable strategy.

The final tactic is to roll down. This entails liquidating the existing bull spread and initiating another bull spread using lower strike prices. One problem with this tactic is that you are initiating the trade with the loss of the original bull spread. The advantage of rolling down is that you are creating a lower break-even point. Table 12.5 compares the result from holding the original bull spread with rolling down by buying the 340 call at 4 3/4 and selling the 345 call at 2 3/4. Remember that the result of the new bull spread includes the loss of 2 7/8 from liquidating the original spread. The most interesting feature of the table is that it shows that you have reduced the profit potential of the new position by the amount you lost on the original spread. This means that you will lock in a loss if you roll down to a new bull spread that has a lower profit potential than the dollar risk on the original spread. As a result, rolling down is usually not the preferable follow-up tactic.

Table 12.5. Bull call spread and rolling down results

Price	Original bull spread	New bull spread
335	-2 7/8	-4 7/8
340	-2 7/8	-4 7/8
345	-2 7/8	-1/8
347 7/8	0	+1/8
350	+2 1/8	+1/8
355	+2 1/8	+1/8

If you expect prices to remain about the same, you could:

> Hold the position
> Liquidate the position

Holding the position is the most common response to this situation. You already know what can happen in terms of risk and reward. You may have already reached the maximum loss point and have nothing more to lose on the trade. If this is the situation, then you might as well hold the position.

On the other hand, liquidating the position is viable if you have a small profit in the trade but are now significantly worried about the possibility of a further down-move. You may want to take the profits you have in the trade and run.

If you expect prices to move lower, you could:

> Hold the position
> Liquidate the position
> Liquidate the long call option if in a bull call spread
> Liquidate the short put option if in a bull put spread

Holding the existing position is the most common tactic.   No further computations of break-evens and risks and rewards are necessary. You know what your risk is and, in fact, you may already have moved to below the point of maximum risk. If this is the case, then you have nothing further to lose on this trade.

Liquidating the position makes sense if you have a small profit in the trade but are now significantly worried about the possibility of a further down-move. You may want to take the profits and eliminate the possibility of further loss.

A more aggressive tactic is to liquidate the long call option if you are in a bull call spread or liquidate the short put option if you are in a bull put spread. This changes the character of the trade to either a short call or a long put. The net effect is that you have liquidated the bull spread and are now taking a more bearish stance on the market. Your rationale may be that the market was only somewhat bullish at higher levels but has become bearish. This may occur because of new information, or because the underlying instrument broke a key price-support level. The problem with this tactic is that it is too easy to rationalize and emotionally make a decision in an effort to double up and catch up. Many traders, when confronted with a losing position, will take on too much risk in an effort to recapture their losses. There is nothing intrinsically wrong with this tactic, but it must be done rationally. Let's look at the bull call spread used in Table 12.3 as an example.

Assume the market dipped to 340 the day after you entered the bull spread. The 345 call is now selling for 2 3/4 and the 350 is selling at 1. Your choice is to stick with the bull call spread or to liquidate the long 345 call. Table 12.6 shows the results at different price levels for these two strategies. Remember that shifting to a short call at this point means that you are starting out with a loss of 2 7/8. This loss is counted in the results of the short call. The price of the 345 call has moved to 2 3/4 and the 350 call is at 1. Notice that, in this example, you can never make a profit. The effect of going naked short the call is to reduce your loss on the original bull spread by capturing additional time premium if the price of the underlying instrument continues lower. The only way you can make a profit by liquidating the long call is if the premium on the short call is larger than the loss on the original bull spread.

Liquidating the short put makes more sense, if you originally put on a bull put spread, because the long put has much greater profit potential than the short call.

Converting a bull call spread into a short call will rarely make sense, but converting it into a long put can often be an attractive tactic if you are now bearish.

Table 12.6.   Bull call spread and short call results

Price	Bull spread	Short call
340	-2 7/8	-1 7/8
345	-2 7/8	-1 7/8
347 7/8	0	-1 7/8
350	+2 1/8	-1 7/8
355	+2 1/8	-4
360	+2 1/8	-9

If the Price of the Underlying Instrument Rises

If you still expect prices to move higher, you could:

> Hold the existing position
> Liquidate the short call option if in a bull call spread
> Liquidate the long put option if in a bull put spread
> Roll up

Holding the existing position is the most common tactic.   No further computations of break-evens and risks and rewards are necessary.   After all, the trade is progressing the way you felt it would.   In general, this is the best course to hold if the price of the underlying instrument has risen and your basic market stance has not changed.

If you feel the market is no more bullish than when you first entered the spread you could liquidate the short call option if you are in a bull call spread, or liquidate the long put option if you are in a bull put spread. This changes the character of the trade to either a long call or a short put. You are now saying that the market is more bullish than you originally thought, and you now want to participate in any further up-side movement. The maximum profit potential may have already been reached on the spread. Let's look at the bull call spread used in Table 12.3 as an example.

Assume the market rallied to 360 the day after you entered the bull spread. The 345 call is now selling for 20 and the 350 is selling at 17. Your choice is between sticking with the bull call spread or liquidating the short 350 call. Table 12.7 shows the results at different price levels for these two strategies. Remember that shifting to a long call at this point means that you are starting out with a locked-in profit of 2 1/8, the maximum profit on this particular spread. This is counted in the results of the long call. Notice that prices must move significantly higher before you will make a profit on the long call. In addition, you now have down-side risk because you are long a call that is far in-the-money.

The alternative is to liquidate the long put. The problem with this is that you have shifted to a position that probably has little time premium in it, and the profits will not be large. You will therefore rarely want to liquidate the long put if you are in bull put spread, but selling the short call can be a viable strategy.

Table 12.7. Bull call spread and long call results

Price	Bull spread	Long call
345	-2 7/8	-17 7/8
350	+2 1/8	-12 7/8
355	+2 1/8	-7 7/8
360	+2 1/8	-2 7/8
365	+2 1/8	+2 1/8
370	+2 1/8	+7 1/8

The final tactic is to roll up. This entails liquidating the existing bull spread and initiating another bull spread using higher strike prices. One advantage with this tactic is that you are initiating the trade with the profit of the original bull spread. The disadvantage of rolling up is that you are creating a higher break-even point. Table 12.8 compares holding the original bull spread with rolling up by buying the 350 call at 13 and selling the 355 call at 10. Remember that the result for the new bull spread includes the profit of 2 1/8 from liquidating the original spread. The most interesting feature of the table is that it shows that you have increased the profit potential of the new position by the amount you gained on the original spread. You will lock in a profit if you roll up to a new bull spread that has a risk that is less than the profit potential on the original spread. As a result, rolling up is usually an attractive follow-up tactic.

Table 12.8.   Bull call spread and rolling up results

Price	Original bull spread	New bull spread
345	-2 7/8	-7/8
350	+2 1/8	-7/8
355	+2 1/8	+4 1/8
360	+2 1/8	+4 1/8
365	+2 1/8	+4 1/8

If you expect prices to remain about the same, you could:

> Hold the position
> Liquidate the position

Holding the position is the most common response to this situation. You already know what can happen in terms of risk and reward. Unfortunately, you may have already reached the point of maximum profit potential.

On the other hand, liquidating the position is a viable tactic if you have reached the point of maximum profit potential. The risk of holding the position is now much higher than the expected reward. You may be better off taking profits now and eliminating your risk.

If you expect prices to move lower, you could:

Hold the position
Liquidate the position
Liquidate the long call option if in a bull call spread
Liquidate the short put option if in a bull put spread

Holding the existing position is the most common tactic. No further computations of break-evens and risks and rewards are necessary. You know what your risk and profit potential are and, in fact, you may already have moved above the point of maximum profit potential. The key is whether you think the price of the underlying instrument will carry below the point of maximum return. Holding the position only makes sense if the risk of lower prices will not hurt the profit in the trade. This will occur only if the price of the underlying instrument has moved significantly over the point of maximum profit potential.

Liquidating the position makes sense if you have a profit in the trade but are now significantly worried about the possibility of a further down-move. You may want to take the profits and eliminate the possibility of further loss.

A more aggressive tactic is to either liquidate the long call option if you are in a bull call spread, or liquidate the short put option if you are in a bull put spread. This changes the character of the trade to either a short call or a long put. The net effect is that you have liquidated the bull spread and are now taking a more bearish stance on the market. Your rationale may be that the market was only somewhat bullish at higher levels but has become bearish, because of new information, or because the underlying instrument broke a key price support level. Look at the bull call spread used in Table 12.3 as an example.

Assume the market rallied to 360 the day after you entered the bull spread. The 345 call is now selling for 20 and the 350 is selling at 17. Your choice is to stick with the bull call spread or liquidate the long 345 call. Table 12.9 shows the results at different price levels for these two strategies. Remember that shifting to a short call at this point means that you are starting out with a loss of 2 7/8. This loss is counted in the results of the short call.   Notice that, in this example, you can never make a profit. The effect of going naked short the call is to reduce your loss on the original bull spread by capturing additional time premium, if the price of the underlying instrument continues lower. The only way you can make a profit by liquidating the long call is if the premium on the short call is larger than the loss on the original bull spread.

Liquidating the short put makes more sense if you originally put on a bull put spread, because the long put has much greater profit potential than the short call.

The net result is that converting a bull call spread into a short call will rarely make sense, but converting it into a long put can often be an attractive tactic if you are now bearish.

Table 12.9.   Bull call spread and short call results

Price	Bull spread	Short call
340	-2 7/8	-1 7/8
345	-2 7/8	-1 7/8
347 7/8	0	-1 7/8
350	+2 1/8	-1 7/8
355	+2 1/8	-4
360	+2 1/8	-9

13

Bear Spreads

A. Strategy
B. Risk/reward
C. Decision structure

STRATEGY

A bear spread is a bearish strategy with both limited risk and profit potential. It is not as bearish as buying a put or selling a call, but the risk is generally lower than buying a put and is significantly lower than selling a call.

A bear spread is either:

> Long a high-strike call and short a low-strike call
> Long a high-strike put and short a low-strike put

This is a popular spread because it usually has a low investment, has limited risk, and compares favorably with other bear strategies. Many investors will take the money they would have invested in long puts and buy bear spreads instead. In many cases, they will end up with greater profit potential if the market moves only moderately lower.

Note the caveat of being only moderately bearish. Bear spreads are a strategy if you are moderately bearish but not if you are very bearish because bear spreads have limited down-side potential. You limit your down-side potential when you buy a bear spread.

Another use of the bear spread is to enhance the profitability of a long call or put. This requires that you are already in a long-call or long-put position.

In any long option trade, you may find yourself in either a profitable or unprofitable situation. If you are holding a profitable long position, you can write a lower strike option to create a bear spread and help protect your profits. In effect, you have limited your profit potential, but you've also limited your risk.

Note that this strategy works for both puts and calls. However, you will be bullish on the market if you are in a profitable call position, but bearish if you are in a profitable put position. This means that your market attitude must turn 180 degrees if you are to use this technique for calls. For puts, this strategy is a signal that you are less bearish than before you switched to a bear spread.

RISK/REWARD

Net Investment Required

The net investment is the price of the option with the lower strike price minus the price of the call with the higher strike price.

This will always be a credit transaction for a bear call spread, because the lower strike call must always be priced lower than the higher strike call. It will also always be a debit transaction for bear put spreads because the higher strike puts must always be priced higher than the lower strike puts.

Let's look at an example. The Major Market Index closes at 350.30, the November 345 call is priced at 10 3/4, and the November 350 call is priced at 7 7/8. Your net investment will be a credit of the difference between the costs of the two options. In this case, you will receive 10 3/4 minus 7 7/8, or 2 7/8. At the same time, the November 345 put is trading at 7 and the November 350 is trading at 9 1/8. Here, the trade would be initiated at a net debit of 2 1/8.

Maximum Return

The maximum return is limited for a bear spread. You will receive the maximum return if the underlying instrument is trading below the lower of the two strike prices when the options expire.

The maximum profit potential for a bear put spread is equal to the higher strike price minus the lower strike price minus the net investment. The maximum profit potential for a bear call spread is the net credit received when the trade is initiated.

Assume you initiated the bear put spread by selling the November 345 put at 7 and buying the November 350 put at 9 1/8 when the MMI was trading at 350.50. You will receive the maximum profit of 2 7/8 if the Major Market Index is below the lower of the two strike prices, in this case, 345. Table 13.1 shows the profit and loss for each of the two options and the net profit or loss for the total position at different prices of the MMI when it expires.

Table 13.1.   Bear put spread results

Price	345 put	350 put	Total profit/loss
330	-8	+10 7/8	+2 7/8
335	-3	+5 7/8	+2 7/8
340	+2	+7/8	+2 7/8
345	+7	-4 1/8	+2 7/8
347 7/8	+7	-7	0
350	+7	-9 1/8	-2 1/8
355	+7	-9 1/8	-2 1/8

Let's add another column to this chart so you can see the difference between this strategy and the outright purchase of a put. In this case, let's assume you bought the November 350 put at 9 1/8. Table 13.2 shows that the purchase of the bear spread is superior to the purchase of a put unless the market drops significantly. The difference is particularly sharp when viewed on an equal-dollar-invested basis. In this example, you could initiate about three bear spreads for less investment than one put.

Table 13.2.   Bear put spread versus put purchase

Price results	345 put	350 put	Total profit/loss	Put
330	-8	+10 7/8	+2 7/8	+10 7/8
335	-3	+5 7/8	+2 7/8	+5 7/8
340	+2	+7/8	+2 7/8	+7/8
345	+7	-4 1/8	+2 7/8	-4 1/8
347 7/8	+7	-7	0	-7
350	+7	-9 1/8	-2 1/8	-9 1/8
355	+7	-9 1/8	-2 1/8	-9 1/8

Maximum Risk

Maximum risk is different for bear call and bear put spreads. For bear put spreads, the maximum risk will occur when the price of the underlying instrument moves above the higher strike price. For a bear call spread, the maximum risk will occur at the point found by adding the lower strike price to the net credit received. The dollar risk is equal to the difference in strike prices minus the credit received.

Table 13.1 showed an example of the maximum risk and the point where it occurs. Table 13.3 shows the same situation for a bear call spread with the 345 call sold for 10 3/4 and the 350 call purchased for 7 7/8.

Table 13.3. Bear call spread results

Price	345 call	350 call	Total profit/loss
340	+10 3/4	-7 7/8	+2 7/8
345	+10 3/4	-7 7/8	+2 7/8
347 7/8	+7 7/8	-7 7/8	0
350	+5 3/4	-7 7/8	-2 1/8
355	+3/4	-2 7/8	-2 1/8

The dollar risk for a bear put spread is the net debit paid to initiate the position. The risk for a bear call spread is the difference between the two strike prices minus the net credit received when the trade was initiated.

The tables above show examples of these calculations, but let's show another two examples here. Assume you sell a Boeing November 55 call at 2, and buy a November 60 call at 3/8, when the stock is trading at 55. Your risk is 3 3/8 (60 - 55 - 1 5/8). Let's look at a bear put spread, where you sell the Boeing November 55 put at 1 5/8 and buy the November 60 put at 5 1/2. The maximum risk for this trade is the net debit of 3 7/8 (5 1/2 - 1 5/8 = 3 7/8).

Break-even Point

The break-even points for bear call and bear put spreads are slightly different. For bear put spreads, the break-even point is the high strike minus net debit paid. For bear call spreads, it is the low-strike price plus net credit received. The tables above give examples of the break-even points.

DECISION STRUCTURE

We mentioned in the **Strategy** section above that there are two possible uses for the bear spread concept: as a trade and as a profit enhancement tool. Both strategies use the same selection and follow-up strategies.

Selection

Bear spreads can be structured to reflect how bearish you are. You can make them as bearish as your market outlook. The most bearish call spread has both legs in-the-money, while the least bearish put spread has both legs in-the-money.

One critical question is whether to select the bear put or the bear call spread. In general, the risk and reward of the two different styles are very close, though some believe that call spreads are slightly more attractive. For example, the ratio of the maximum profit potential to the dollar risk will tend to be slightly higher for bear call spreads than for bear put spreads. In addition, bear call spreads are credit transactions.

These advantages don't come free. One disadvantage with call spreads is that they are liable for early exercise if you are short an in-the-money option. The more bearish you are, the more chance of early exercise. Thus, you may be exercised before having a chance to make the maximum profit.

One problem with bear put spreads is that puts tend to be less liquid than calls. As a result, the bid/ask spread may be larger, and you may have more trouble entering or exiting your trade in the quantity you want.

Another negative feature of bear call spreads is that time decay is working against the bear call spreader. Time is usually working in favor of the bear call spreader due to the usually greater decline in the time premium of the short call than the long call. However, note that time is working against the bear put spread because the long put's time premium is likely to be decaying faster than the short put's time premium.

Another consideration for selecting a bear spread is commissions, which tend to be a larger percentage of the potential profit than with other option strategies. Be sure to consider the cost of commissions before selecting a bear spread over other bearish strategies, and before selecting the strike price.

Bear spreads can be selected by looking at their maximum risk/reward weighted by their chances of occurring, based on the implied volatility or your expected volatility. The first step in this procedure is to list the ratio of maximum profit potential versus the maximum dollar risk of all possible bear spreads. Step two is to weight the results by their chances of occurring, as determined by either the implied volatility or your expected volatility. This will give you an expected return on all the bear spreads for that instrument. Unfortunately, this technique requires a computer to go through the myriad of computations.

If the Price of the Underlying Instrument Drops

If you expect prices to move higher, you could:

> Hold the position
> Liquidate the position
> Liquidate the short call option if in a bear call spread
> Liquidate the long put option if in a bear put spread

Holding the existing position is the most common tactic. No further computations of break-evens and risks and rewards are necessary. You know what your risk and profit potential are and, in fact, you may already have moved above the point of maximum profit potential. The key is whether you think the price of the underlying instrument will carry above the point of maximum return. Holding the position only makes sense if the risk of higher prices will not hurt the profit in the trade. This will occur only if the price of the underlying instrument has moved significantly below the point of maximum profit potential.

Liquidating the position makes sense if you have a profit in the trade but are now significantly worried about the possibility of a further up-move. You may want to take the profits and eliminate the possibility of further loss.

A more aggressive tactic is to either liquidate the short call option if you are in a bear call spread, or liquidate the long put option if you are in a bear put spread. This changes the character of the trade to either a short put or a long call. You have liquidated the bear spread and are now taking a more bullish stance on the market. Your rationale may be that the market was only somewhat bearish at lower levels but has become bullish, because of new information, or because the underlying instrument broke a key price resistance level. Let's use the bear call spread from Table 13.3 as an example, and compare it with the liquidation of the short call.

Assume the market dropped to 340 the day after you entered the bear spread. The 345 call is now selling for 2 3/4 and the 350 is selling at 1. Your choice is to stick with the bear call spread, or to liquidate the short 345 call. Table 13.4 shows the results at different price levels for these two tactics. Remember that shifting to a long call at this point means that you will have picked up the maximum profit on the bear spread. As a result, you will be starting out with a profit of 2 7/8. This profit is included in the results of the long call.

The interesting feature of this tactic is that you may be able to lock in a profit, though it will be lower than the profit you had when you initiated the long call. You still have the potential to gain additional profits if the market climbs high enough. This feature will occur if the premium on the long call is less than the profit on the bear spread.

The alternative to liquidating the short call is to liquidate the long put, leaving a short put. Although this is riskier, there is usually enough premium in the short put to make the trade attractive. Both alternatives should be examined.

Table 13.4. Bear call spread and long call results

Price	Bear call spread	Long call
340	+2 7/8	+1 7/8
345	+2 7/8	+1 7/8
350	-2 1/8	+1 7/8
355	-2 1/8	+6 7/8
360	-2 1/8	+11 7/8

If you expect prices to remain about the same, you could:

> Hold the position
> Liquidate the position

Holding the position is the most common response to this situation. You already know what can happen in terms of risk and reward. Unfortunately, you may have already reached the point of maximum profit potential.

On the other hand, liquidating the position is a viable tactic if you have reached the point of maximum profit potential. The risk of holding the position is now much higher than the expected reward. You may be better off to take profits now and eliminate your risk.

If you still expect prices to move lower, you could:

Hold the existing position
Liquidate
Liquidate the short put option if in a bear put spread
Liquidate the long call option if in a bear call spread
Roll down

Holding the existing position is the most common tactic. No further computations of break-evens and risks and rewards are necessary. After all, the trade is progressing the way you felt it would. In general, this is the best course to hold if the price of the underlying instrument has risen and your basic market stance has not changed.

Liquidating the position makes sense if you have a small profit in the trade, but are now significantly worried about the possibility of a sharp move higher. You may want to take the profits and eliminate the possibility of further loss.

If you feel the market is now more bearish than when you first entered the spread, you could either liquidate the short put option if you are in a bear put spread or liquidate the long call option if you are in a bear call spread. This changes the character of the trade to either a long put or a short call. You are now saying that the market is more bearish than you originally thought, and you now want to participate in further down-side movement. The maximum profit potential may have already been reached on the spread. The bear put spread used back in Table 13.1 is an example.

Assume that the market dropped to 340 the day after you entered the bear spread. The 345 put is now selling for 17, and the 350 put is selling at 20. Your choice is to stick with the bear put spread, or to liquidate the short 345 put. Table 13.5 shows the results at different price levels for these two tactics. Shifting to a long put at this point means that you are starting out with a locked-in profit of 2 7/8, the maximum profit on the original spread. This is counted in the results of the long put. Notice that prices must move significantly lower before you will make a profit on the long put. In addition, you now have significant up-side risk because you are long a put that is far in-the-money.

The alternative is to liquidate the long call. The problem with this is that you have shifted to a position that probably has little time premium in it and the profits will not be very large. You will therefore rarely want to liquidate the long call if you are in a bear call spread, but selling the short put can be a viable strategy.

Table 13.5.   Bear put spread versus put purchase

Price	Spread profit/loss	Put result
325	+2 7/8	+7 7/8
330	+2 7/8	+2 7/8
335	+2 7/8	-2 1/8
340	+2 7/8	-7 1/8
345	+2 7/8	-12 1/8
350	-2 1/8	-17 1/8
355	-2 1/8	-17 1/8

The final tactic is to roll down. This entails liquidating the existing bear spread and initiating another bear spread using lower strike prices. One advantage with this tactic is that you are initiating the trade with the profit of the original bear spread. The disadvantage of rolling down is that you are creating a lower break-even point. Table 13.6 compares holding the original bear call spread shown in Table 13.3 with rolling down by buying the 345 call at 8 3/4 and selling the 340 call at 5 3/4. Remember that the result for the new bear spread includes the profit of 2 7/8 from liquidating the original spread. The most interesting feature of the table is that it shows that you have increased the profit potential of the new position by the amount you gained on the original spread. This means that you will lock in a profit if you roll up to a new bull spread that has a risk that is less than the profit potential on the original spread. In this example, you could still lose money, but your risk would be small and you would be increasing the profit potential if you are still bearish.

Table 13.6. Bear call spread and rolling down results

Price	Original bear spread	New bear spread
325	+2 7/8	+5 7/8
330	+2 7/8	+5 7/8
335	+2 7/8	+5 7/8
340	+2 7/8	+4 7/8
345	+2 7/8	-1/8
350	-2 1/8	-1/8
355	-2 1/8	-1/8

If the Price of the Underlying Instrument Rises

If you still expect prices to move higher, you could:

> Hold the existing position
> Liquidate the short call option if in a bear call spread
> Liquidate the long put option if in a bear put spread

Holding the existing position is the most common tactic. No further computations of break-evens and risks and rewards are necessary. You know what your risk is and, in fact, you may already have moved to above the point of maximum risk. If this is the case, you have nothing further to lose on this trade.

A more aggressive tactic is to either liquidate the short call option if you are in a bear call spread, or liquidate the long put option if you are in a bear put spread. This changes the character of the trade to either a short put or a long call. The net effect is that you have liquidated the bear spread and are now taking a more bullish stance on the market. Your rationale may be that the market was only somewhat bearish at lower levels but has become bullish. This may occur because of new information, or because the underlying instrument broke a key price resistance level. The problem with this tactic is that it is too easy to rationalize and emotionally make a decision in an effort to double up and catch up. Many traders, when confronted with a losing position, will take on too much risk in an effort to recapture their losses. The net effect is that there is nothing intrinsically wrong with this tactic, but it must be done rationally. Let's use the bear call spread from Table 13.3 as an example and compare this with the liquidation of the short call.

Assume the market rose to 360 the day after you entered the bear spread. The 345 call is now selling for 20 and the 350 is selling at 17. Your choice is to stick with the bear call spread or to liquidate the short 345 call. Table 13.7 shows the results at different price levels for these two tactics. Notice that prices must move significantly higher before you will make a profit on the long call. In addition, you now have significant down-side risk because you are long a call that is far in-the-money.

The alternative to liquidating the short call is to liquidate the long put, leaving a short put. Although this is riskier, there is usually enough premium in the short put to make the trade attractive. Both alternatives should be examined.

Table 13.7. Bear call spread and long call results

Price	Bear call spread	Long call
350	-2 1/8	-19 1/8
355	-2 1/8	-14 1/8
360	-2 1/8	-9 1/8
365	-2 1/8	-4 1/8
370	-2 1/8	+7/8
375	-2 1/8	+5 7/8

If you expect prices to remain about the same, you could:

Hold the position
Liquidate the position

Holding the position is the most common response to this situation. You already know what can happen in terms of risk and reward. You may have already reached the maximum loss point and have nothing more to lose on the trade. If this is the situation, then you might as well hold the position.

On the other hand, liquidating the position is a viable tactic if you have a small loss in the trade but are now significantly worried about the possibility of a further up-move. In effect, you are eliminating the position for a small loss rather than a larger loss.

If you still expect prices to move lower, you could:

> Hold the existing position
> Liquidate the short put option if in a bear put spread
> Liquidate the long call option if in a bear call spread

Holding the position is the most common response to this situation. You already know what can happen in terms of risk and reward. You may have already reached the maximum loss point and have nothing more to lose on the trade. If this is the situation, then you might as well hold the position.

If you feel the market is still bearish, you could liquidate the short put option if you are in a bear put spread, or else liquidate the long call option if you are in a bear call spread. This changes the character of the trade to either a long put or a short call. The net effect is that you have shifted your position from somewhat bearish to very bearish. The bear put spread used back in Table 13.1 is an example.

Assume that the market rose to 360 the day after you entered the bear spread. The 345 put is now selling for 5 3/4, and the 350 put is selling at 2. Your choice is to stick with the bear put spread or to liquidate the short 345 put. Table 13.8 shows the results at different price levels for these two tactics. Shifting to a long put at this point means that you are starting out with a loss of 2 1/8 on the original spread. This loss is counted in the results of the long put. Note that prices must move significantly lower before you will make a profit on the long put. However, your up-side risk is minimal because the put is out-of-the-money and the premium cost is low.

The alternative is to liquidate the long call. The problem with this is that you have shifted to a position that probably has little time premium in it and the profits will not be very large. You will therefore rarely want to liquidate the long call if you are in bear call spread, but selling the short put can be a viable strategy.

Table 13.8.   Bear put spread versus put purchase

Price	Spread profit/loss	Put result
335	+2 7/8	+12 7/8
340	+2 7/8	+5 7/8
345	+2 7/8	+7/8
350	-2 1/8	-4 1/8
355	-2 1/8	-4 1/8
360	-2 1/8	-4 1/8

14

Butterfly Spreads

A. Strategy
B. Equivalent strategy
C. Risk/reward
D. Decision structure

STRATEGY

You can initiate both long and short butterfly spreads. Butterfly spreads are usually considered neutral strategies that can be constructed with either puts or calls. However, butterflies can be constructed that have a bullish or bearish bias.

A long butterfly is constructed by:

> Buying one low-strike option
> Selling two medium-strike options
> Buying one high-strike option

A short butterfly is constructed by:

> Selling one low-strike option
> Buying two medium-strike options
> Selling one high-strike option

Butterflies are usually considered neutral strategies. Long butterflies look for the market to be stable, with little price movement. The short butterfly looks for prices to move sharply in either direction. The long butterfly is neutral in that it does not look for prices to move very far. The short butterfly is neutral in that it looks for prices to move significantly in one direction or the other. A person putting on a short butterfly doesn't have to have an opinion on the future direction of the market, but does have to expect a move in some direction.

A bullish butterfly has strike prices where the middle-strike price is above the current market price of the underlying instrument. Bearish butterflies have the middle-strike below the current market price. The price of the underlying instrument will have to rise or fall toward the middle-strike price before the maximum profit potential will be realized.

However, there are usually better bull or bear strategies than constructing bull or bear butterflies. As a result, butterflies are nearly always initiated with a neutral market bias.

EQUIVALENT STRATEGY

There are two equivalent strategies for the long butterfly:

1. Buy a low-strike put, short a medium-strike put, short a medium-strike call, and buy a high-strike call
2. Buy a low-strike call, short a medium-strike call, short a medium-strike put, and buy a high-strike put.

There are two equivalent strategies for the short butterfly:

1. Short a low-strike put, buy a medium-strike put, buy a medium-strike call, and short a high-strike call
2. Short a low-strike call, buy a medium-strike call, buy a medium-strike put, and short a high-strike put.

Note that the distance between the low and medium and the medium and high strikes must be equal. It should also be noted that the equivalent strategies are simply combinations of bull and bear spreads. Thus, you can leg into butterflies by initiating appropriate bull or bear spreads.

RISK/REWARD

Break-even Points

There are two break-evens for each of the butterflies. The break-even formulas below assume that the distance between the middle strike price to the highest and lowest strike prices are equidistant.

For the long butterfly:

> Up-side break-even = highest strike price - net debit
> Down-side break-even = lowest strike price + net debit

For the short butterfly:

> Up-side break-even = highest strike price - net credit
> Down-side break-even = lowest strike price + net credit

Let's look at an example of the two break-evens for a long butterfly. Assume that Monsanto is trading at 69 3/4 and you want to trade the January options. The 65 strike is trading at 6 1/4, the 70 strike is at 4, and the 75 strike last traded at 2. Construct your long butterfly by buying 1 of the 65 strikes for a debit of 6 1/4, selling 2 of the 70 strikes for a credit of 8, and buying 1 of the 75 strikes for a debit of 2. The net debit on the trade is 1/4 (-6 1/4 + 8 - 2 = -1/4). The up-side break-even point is the highest strike price, 75, minus the net debit, 1/4, or 74 3/4. The down-side break-even is the lowest strike price, 65, plus the net debit, 1/4, or 65 1/4.

Assume you initiated a short butterfly with the following prices:

> Dun & Bradstreet stock = 105 1/2
> November 100 call = 6 3/4
> November 105 call = 3
> November 110 call = 1 1/4

This short butterfly would be initiated for a net credit of $2 (+6 3/4 - 6 + 1/14 = 2). The up-side break-even is the highest strike price, $110, minus the net credit, $2, or $108. The down-side break-even is the lowest strike price, $100, plus the net credit, $2, or $102.

Maximum Risk

The maximum risk for a long butterfly is the net debit of the spread, and occurs outside of the break-even points. The maximum risk for a short butterfly is the difference between the middle strike price and one of the outer strike prices (assuming that the middle strike price is equidistant from the outer strike prices) minus the net credit received when the trade is initiated.

For example, you have initiated a short butterfly using the $45, $50, and $55 strike prices and received $1 in premium. Your maximum risk is the difference between the middle option strike price, $50, and either of the two outer strikes, $45, minus the net credit of $1 for a total of $4 ($50 - $45 - $1 = $4).

Profit Potential

The maximum profit for a long butterfly is the distance between the middle strike and one of the outer strikes minus the net debit. This assumes equal distance between the three strikes. The maximum profit will be achieved at the middle strike.

The maximum profit for a short butterfly is the net credit. This will be achieved at the points represented by the value of the net credit plus the up-side break-even point, or at the down-side break-even point minus the value of the net credit.

Assume a long butterfly of December Telex options with strikes of $50, $55, and $60. The three entry prices are 7, 3 1/2, and 1 5/8, respectively. The net debit is 1 5/8. Thus, the maximum profit potential for this spread is the distance between the middle strike and one of the two outer strikes, 5, minus the net debit, 1 5/8, for a total of 3 3/8.

DECISION STRUCTURE

Selection

One key to selecting a butterfly is the cost. The best long butterfly is the cheapest butterfly. The least expensive butterfly will have the lowest dollar risk and the widest range of break-even points. You should try to enter the long butterfly at a premium cost of less than 10 percent of the distance between two of the strike prices. For example, you are interested in buying a butterfly in a stock with strike prices at $50 and $55. This rule of thumb suggests that you should consider purchasing the long butterfly only if you can buy it for less than .50. An option evaluation program is useful for identifying possibly under-priced options that can be used to construct a long butterfly.

A second criteria is that you will want to select the outer strike prices to be beyond the expected range of the underlying instrument for the time you will be in the trade. You will therefore be selecting those underlying instruments that you expect to be stagnant.

The converse is true with a short butterfly. You are looking for a situation that has over-priced options. The profit potential of the trade is entirely the net price you receive for the option. In addition, you are looking for a situation where the underlying instrument has an excellent chance of moving in either direction. You are looking for an underlying instrument you expect to move beyond the range defined by the two outer strike prices.

Another consideration is volatility. Rising volatility will help a long butterfly but hurt a short butterfly. This is because the volatility will increase the price of the options beyond the initial price, all things being equal.

The final consideration is the selection of the middle strike price. The common practice is to select the at-the-money option as the middle strike price. However, selecting a higher or lower strike price will turn the butterfly into a bull or bear strategy. A higher strike price turns a long butterfly into a bull strategy, whereas a lower strike price will turn it into a bear strategy. A higher strike price turns a short butterfly into a bear strategy, whereas a lower strike price turns the short butterfly into a bull strategy.

If the Price of the Underlying Instrument Drops

The tactics for long and short butterflies are opposite. In general, short butterflies are not popular strategies because of the limited profit potential. Most traders will focus on similar strategies that usually present a better risk/reward ratio. Also, the follow-up tactics of short butterflies are the flip side of long butterflies. This means that you can simply take the opposite side of the long butterfly tactics. As a result, we will focus only on the tactics for long butterflies.

If you expect prices to move higher, you could:

> Hold the current position
> Convert to bull spread
> Convert to long call(s) or short put(s)

Holding the current position makes sense if the price of the underlying instrument will stay within the limits of the two break-even points. For example, prices may have dropped to below the lower break-even point. Now that you are more bullish, it makes sense to hold the position, looking for it to climb back into the profit zone.

On the other hand, if you are so bullish that you think the price will go above the up-side break-even, you will still want to hold the position and liquidate it when it moves to the middle strike price.

One interesting tactic is to convert the position into a bull spread. This tactic is basically saying that you are now longer neutral on the market but have become bullish. Let's look at an example of the differences in results using this approach versus leaving the original position untouched. Table 14.1 shows these results. Assume that the trade was initiated with the following prices:

> OEX = 230.00
> December 220 call = 15 1/2
> December 225 call = 13
> December 230 call = 10 3/4
> Net debit of 1/4

However, the market has dropped to 225, you have switched to the bull camp, and prices are now:

> OEX = 225
> December 220 call = 9 7/8
> December 225 call = 7 1/2
> December 230 call = 5

Table 14.1. Long butterfly and bull call spread results

Price	Long butterfly	Bull spread
220	-1/4	-2 3/8
225	+4 3/4	+2 5/8
230	-1/4	+2 5/8

Notice that you will make more money sticking with the long butterfly if the market stabilizes, but you'll make more money on shifting to the bull spread if the market moves higher. The drawback to the shift to the bull spread is that you are also giving up the miniscule risk of the long butterfly if the market continues lower.

The final and most bullish alternative is to convert the position to either a long call or a short put. This entails liquidating three of the four options in the butterfly. Let's continue with the example above. Table 14.2 shows the results of keeping the original butterfly spread and moving to the long 220 call at 9 7/8.

Table 14.2. Long butterfly and long call results

Price	Long butterfly	Long call
220	-1/4	-9 7/8
225	+4 3/4	-4 7/8
230	-1/4	+1/8
235	-1/4	+5 1/8

The net result is that you must have become very bullish to want to shift to a long call over holding the existing butterfly. The risks and the rewards are significantly higher for the long call than for the butterfly.

The alternative to a long call is to hold one of the short puts. This will have less profit potential than the long call but has more risk. The main advantage is that you will make money at a lower level compared with the long call. Another advantage is that you are selling time premium rather than buying time premium.

If you look for prices to stabilize, you could:

> Hold the position
> Liquidate the position
> Roll down

Holding the current position makes sense if the price of the underlying instrument will stay within the limits of the two break-even points. For example, prices may have dropped to just above the lower break-even point. It makes sense to hold the position to take the small profit.

Liquidating the position can make sense if prices have dropped to outside the profit zone and if you can limit your losses to something less than the initial risk. Since the risk in long butterflies is usually very low, most investors do not liquidate their existing position and, instead, wait for the price to rally.

A final possibility in this situation is to roll down. This entails liquidating the current butterfly and initiating a new position with lower strike prices. You may be taking a loss on the initial position looking to increase your profit potential if prices stay at their current position. Table 14.3 shows the results for an example.

Table 14.3. Long butterfly and roll down results

Price	Original butterfly	New butterfly
215	-1/4	+1
220	-1/4	+6
225	+4 3/4	+1
230	-1/4	+1

If you look for prices to move lower, you could:

> Hold the position
> Liquidate the position
> Convert to bear spread
> Convert to short call(s) or long put(s)
> Roll down

Holding the current position makes sense only if no other tactic looks attractive. In other words, you may want to sit on your small loss rather than take the additional risk of other tactics.

Liquidating the position can make sense if prices have dropped to outside the profit zone and if you can limit your losses to something less than the initial risk.   Since the risk in long butterflies is usually very low, most investors do not liquidate their existing position and, instead, wait for the price to rally.

Another alternative is to convert the position into a bear spread. This tactic is basically saying that you are no longer neutral on the market, but have become bearish. Let's look at an example of the differences in results from using the long 230 call/short 225 call bear spread versus leaving the original position untouched. Table 14.4 shows these results at expiration. Assume that the trade was initiated with the following prices with a net debit of 1/4:
OEX = 230.00
December 220 call = 15 1/2
December 225 call = 13
December 230 call = 10 3/4

However, the market has dropped to 225, you have switched to the bear side, and prices are now:

OEX = 225
December 220 call = 9 7/8
December 225 call = 7 1/2
December 230 call = 5

Table 14.4.   Long butterfly and bear call spread results

Price	Long butterfly	Bear spread
215	-1/4	+2 3/8
220	-1/4	+2 3/8
225	+4 3/4	-2 5/8
230	-1/4	-2 5/8

Notice that you will make more money sticking with the long butterfly if the market stabilizes but will make more money on shifting to the bear spread if the market moves lower.   The drawback to the shift to the bear spread is that you are also giving up the miniscule risk of the long butterfly if the market continues higher.

The most bearish alternative is to convert the position to either a short call or a long put.   This entails liquidating three of the four options in the butterfly.   Let's continue with the example above. Table 14.5 shows the results of keeping the original butterfly spread versus moving to the short 225 call at 7 1/2.   This shows that shorting the call at the middle strike can be an attractive alternative if you have turned bearish.   Note, however, that the short call has greater risk if the market rallies significantly.

Table 14.5. Long butterfly and short call results

Price	Long butterfly	Short call
215	-1/4	+7 1/2
220	-1/4	+7 1/2
225	+4 3/4	+7 1/2
230	-1/4	+2 1/2
235	-1/4	-2 1/2
240	-1/4	-7 1/2

The alternative to a short call is to hold a long put if you have initiated a butterfly using puts. This will have greater profit potential than the short call, but also more risk. One main problem with converting to the put is that the break-even point is lower than with the short call. Another disadvantage is that you are selling time premium rather than buying time premium.

A final possibility in this situation is to roll down. This entails liquidating the current butterfly and initiating a new position with lower strike prices. You may be taking a loss on the initial position, looking to increase your profit potential if prices stay at their current position. Table 14.6 shows an example of rolling down so that the middle strike is at-the-money. In this case, you are rolling down to the 215, 220, and 225 strikes with prices of 11 1/4, 9 7/8, and 7 1/2, respectively. A more bearish tactic would be to lower the strike prices even further.

Table 14.6. Long butterfly and roll down results

Price	Original butterfly	New butterfly
215	-1/4	+1
220	-1/4	+6
225	+4 3/4	+1
230	-1/4	+1

If the Price of the Underlying Instrument Rises

If you expect prices to move higher, you could:

> Liquidate
> Convert to bull spread
> Convert to short put(s) or long call(s)
> Roll up

Liquidating the position can make sense if prices have rallied to outside the profit zone and if you can limit your losses to something less than the initial risk. Since the risk in long butterflies is usually very low, most investors do not liquidate their existing position and, instead, wait for the price to slump back to the profit zone.

One interesting tactic is to convert the position into a bull spread. This tactic is basically saying that you are no longer neutral on the market but have become bullish. Let's look at an example of the differences in results using this approach versus leaving the original position untouched. Table 14.7 shows these results. Assume that the trade was initiated with the following prices:

> OEX = 230.00
> December 220 call = 15 1/2
> December 225 call = 13
> December 230 call = 10 3/4
> Net debit of 1/4

However, the market has jumped to 235, you have switched to the bull camp, and prices are now:

> OEX = 235
> December 220 call = 21 1/8
> December 225 call = 18 1/2
> December 230 call = 16 1/2

Table 14.7. Long butterfly and bull call spread results

Price	Long butterfly	Bull spread
220	-1/4	-2 5/8
225	+4 3/4	+2 3/8
230	-1/4	+2 3/8
235	-1/4	+2 3/8
240	-1/4	+2 3/8

Notice that you will make more money sticking with the long butterfly if the market stabilizes, but you'll make more money on shifting to the bull spread if the market moves higher. The drawback to the shift to the bull spread is that you are also giving up the miniscule risk of the long butterfly if the market continues lower.

The final and most bullish alternative is to convert the position to either a long call or a short put. This entails liquidating three of the four options in the butterfly. Let's continue with the example above. Table 14.8 shows the results of keeping the original butterfly spread and moving to the long 220 call at 21 1/8.

Table 14.8. Long butterfly and long call results

Price	Long butterfly	Long call
215	-1/4	-21 1/8
220	-1/4	-21 1/8
225	+4 3/4	-16 1/8
230	-1/4	-11 1/8
235	-1/4	-6 1/8
240	-1/4	-1 1/8
245	-1/4	+3 7/8

The net result is that you must have become very bullish to want to shift to a long call over holding the existing butterfly. The risks and the rewards are significantly higher for the long call than the butterfly. This example uses the 220 call and understates the attractiveness of shifting to the other call, the 230. The 230 call would have less premium and therefore less risk. Nonetheless, you still need to be much more bullish to be induced to shift to the long call strategy.

The alternative to a long call is to hold one of the short puts. This has less profit potential than the long call and more risk. The main advantage is that you will make money at a lower level compared with the long call. Another advantage is that you are selling, rather than buying, time premium.

A final possibility in this situation is to roll up. This entails liquidating the current butterfly and initiating a new position with higher strike prices. You may take a loss on the initial position, looking to increase your profit potential if prices stay at their current position. Table 14.9 shows an example of rolling up so that the middle strike is at-the-money. In this case, you are rolling up to the 225, 230, and 235 strikes with prices of 12 1/2, 10, and 8 1/4, respectively. A more bullish tactic is to raise the strike prices even further.

Table 14.9. Long butterfly and roll up results

Price	Original butterfly	New butterfly
220	-1/4	-3/4
225	+4 3/4	-3/4
230	-1/4	+4 1/4
235	-1/4	-3/4

You have basically shifted your profit zone to a higher level at a cost of additional commissions and probably a loss on the original butterfly. Nonetheless, this is a viable tactic if you are convinced that prices will not change much from their current level.

If you look for prices to stabilize, you could:

Hold the position
Liquidate the position
Roll up

Holding the current position makes sense if the price of the underlying instrument will stay within the limits of the two break-even points. Otherwise, you should consider one of the other tactics.

Liquidating the position can make sense if prices have risen to outside the profit zone and if you can limit your losses to something less than the initial risk. Since the risk in long butterflies is usually very low, most investors do not liquidate their existing position and, instead, wait for the price to drop back into the profit zone.

Rolling up is also sensible if you are looking for prices to stabilize. You will be swapping a small loss in the original butterfly plus some commissions for a greater chance at profit at current levels. Table 14.6 and the discussion surrounding it show the potential value of this tactic.

If you look for prices to move lower, you could:

> Hold position
> Convert to bear spread
> Convert to short call(s) or long put(s)

Holding the current position makes sense if the price of the underlying instrument will stay within the limits of the two break-even points. For example, prices may have rallied to above the upper break-even point. Now that you are more bearish, it makes sense to hold the position, looking for it to slump back into the profit zone.

On the other hand, if you are so bearish that you think the price will go to below the down-side break-even, you will still want to hold the position and liquidate it when it moves to the middle strike price.

Liquidating the position can make sense if prices have rallied to outside the profit zone, and if you can limit your losses to something less than the initial risk.   Since the risk in long butterflies is usually very low, most investors do not liquidate their existing position and, instead, wait for the price to drop.

Another alternative is to convert the position into a bear spread. This tactic is basically saying that you are no longer neutral on the market but have become bearish.   Let's look at an example of the differences in results from using the long 230 call/short 225 call bear spread versus leaving the original position untouched. Table 14.10 shows these results at expiration. Assume that the trade was initiated with the following prices:

OEX = 230.00
December 220 call = 15 1/2
December 225 call = 13
December 230 call = 10 3/4
Net debit of 1/4

However, the market has jumped to 235, you have switched to the bear side, and prices are now:

OEX = 235
December 225 call = 18
December 230 call = 15 3/4

Table 14.10.   Long butterfly and bear call spread results

Price	Long butterfly	Bear spread
220	-1/4	+2 1/4
225	+4 3/4	+2 1/4
230	-1/4	-2 3/4
235	-1/4	-2 3/4

Notice that you will make more money sticking with the long butterfly if the market stabilizes, but you will make more money on shifting to the bear spread if the market moves lower.   The drawback to the shift to the bear spread is that you are also giving up the miniscule risk of the long butterfly if the market continues higher.

The final and most bearish alternative is to convert the position to either a short call or a long put. This entails liquidating three of the four options in the butterfly. Let's continue with the example above. Table 14.11 shows the results of keeping the original butterfly spread versus moving to the short 225 call at 18. Shorting the call at the middle strike can be an attractive alternative if you have turned bearish. Note, however, that the short call has greater risk if the market rallies significantly.

Table 14.11. Long butterfly and short call results

Price	Long butterfly	Short call
220	-1/4	+18
225	+4 3/4	+18
230	-1/4	+13
235	-1/4	+8
240	-1/4	+3
245	-1/4	-2
250	-1/4	-7

The alternative to a short call would be to hold a long put if you had initiated a butterfly using puts. This will have greater profit potential than the short call, but more risk. One main problem with converting to the put is that the break-even point is lower than with the short call. Another disadvantage is that you are buying rather than selling time premium.

15

Calendar Spreads

A. Strategy
B. Risk/reward
C. Decision structure

STRATEGY

Calendar spreads are constructed by buying or selling a put or call in one expiration month and taking the opposite position in a farther expiration month.

Calendar spreads can be constructed that are bullish or bearish. There are two ways to construct neutral calendar spreads.

A neutral calendar spread can be constructed by selling a nearby at-the-money option and buying a farther expiration contract with the same strike. This strategy is used when you are looking for prices to remain stable but want to capture the time decay of the nearby option. For example, you could sell the United Airlines (UAL) November 60 calls for 2 and buy the February 60 calls for 3 7/8 when the price of UAL is 59.

A second type of neutral calendar spread, called a reverse calendar spread, is constructed by buying the nearby option and selling the far option. A large price move in the underlying instrument is required before the reverse calendar will profit. Unfortunately, the decay in the time premium works against the trade, rarely making it attractive. As a result, we will not spend any more time on this strategy.

A bullish calendar spread can be constructed by using a strike price above the current market price. For example, the current price of the underlying instrument is 50, and you sell a nearby option and buy a far option, both with a strike of 60.

A bearish calendar spread can be constructed by using a strike price below the current price of the underlying instrument. With a current instrument price of $50, you would sell a nearby call and buy a far call with a strike of $40.

RISK/REWARD

Break-even Point

Unfortunately, we cannot precisely ascertain the break-even points because we do not know the time decay. Changes in the implied volatility can also have a big impact on the break-even point. In addition, the time premium changes as the price of the underlying instrument changes. One change occurs as the price of the underlying instrument moves past different strike prices. For example, you may initiate a position at one strike price, which will have the greatest time value, but, as the price of the underlying moves higher or lower, the at-the-money option will change to different strike prices, thus reducing the time value of the original option. Assume that you initiate a calendar spread using the options on Treasury-bond futures using the September and December 96 00/32 strikes when the price of the underlying futures contract is 96 5/32. These options, being the at-the-money options, will have the greatest time premium. Their time premium will contract if the price of the bonds moves significantly in either direction.

Investment Required

The investment for a calendar spread is the net debit. Assume the following prices:

> Exxon = 67
> October 65 call = 2 1/4
> November 65 call = 2 3/4

The calendar spread would be constructed by buying the November 65 call for 2 3/4 and selling the October 65 call for 2 1/4. The net debit and the net investment will be .50 (2 1/4 - 2 3/4 = -1/2).

Maximum Risk

The maximum risk in a calendar spread is the net debit. In the Exxon example given above, the maximum you could lose on this trade would be .50. Unfortunately, you cannot pinpoint precisely the points of maximum risk because you cannot know the amount of time decay on the far option. At the expiration of the nearby contract, you will still be holding another option. The time premium on the far option will be affected by such factors as time remaining before expiration, implied volatility, and distance from the current price of the underlying instrument. As a result, you can only estimate the maximum risk in the trade by making assumptions about the future time premium of the far option in the calendar spread.

This means that you should have some type of options evaluation model and a market opinion to help estimate where your risk will be at its maximum.

Profit Potential

The profit potential for a calendar spread is unlimited but cannot be reduced to a formula. This is because of the myriad of possible price scenarios and the many possible responses to those scenarios. For example, you may initiate a calendar spread, see the price drop to below the nearby strike price, the nearby option expire worthless, and then the market rally. You could liquidate the whole trade at the lower level or hang onto the far call looking for a rally. This example shows making a profit on both a short nearby option and a long far option. But the price scenario could be different and your responses to the market action could vary dramatically. As a result, the description of the profit potential cannot be neatly packaged. Nonetheless, Figure 15.1 shows an example of the option chart for a neutral calendar spread.

CALENDAR SPREAD
Figure 15.1

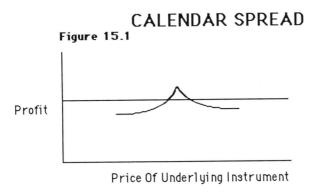

Profit

Price Of Underlying Instrument

DECISION STRUCTURE

Selection

An important goal of a calendar spread is to capture the time premium of the nearby expiration option. This means the ideal situation is to sell a nearby option with a high time premium and a high implied volatility and to sell a far contract with relatively low time value and relatively low implied volatility. Unfortunately, this ideal situation is rarely achieved.

As a practical matter, this means that initiation should take place when time decay is at its greatest. You should therefore be looking to initiate this trade just as the option time premium is beginning to descend rapidly. The formula for estimating the time decay was given in Chapter 2 - The Fundamentals Of Options.

Neutral calendar spreads are initiated close to at-the-money. This gives the greatest time decay to the nearby option while giving the greatest chance of movement to help the far option.

For bull and bear calendar spreads, you should put the point of maximum profit potential at your price objective. Thus, you may expect the price of Colgate to rally to 45 from its current price of 38 1/2. You should therefore sell the nearby option with a strike of 45 and buy the same strike price in a farther option.

Another factor to consider is the expiration month. Usually, traders use the two nearest expirations. These options have the greatest liquidity, a major advantage. However, you should look at your market opinion and then decide which expirations make the most sense.

If the Price of the Underlying Instrument Drops

If you are looking for higher prices, you could:

> Liquidate the position
> Liquidate the short option

You could liquidate the position if you are satisfied with the profits on the trade after the decline in prices. You may also want to liquidate the trade if you are looking for higher prices and there is too much time until the expiration of the nearby option. Remember that the best thing that could happen would be a drop in prices, with the nearby option expiring, followed by a big rally. You would then make the maximum on both legs of the spread.

A more aggressive tactic is to liquidate the short call. You have then shifted your position to a long call. This means that you will need the market to trade significantly higher before you make a profit on the trade, but you now have much more profit potential.

If you are looking for stable prices, you could:

> Hold if within the expected profit zone
> Liquidate if below expected break-even
> Roll down

You could hold the position if prices have not moved to below your expected break-even at expiration of the first contract.

Alternately, you could liquidate the position if the price of the underlying instrument has fallen below the expected break-even point.

A third choice would be to roll down to a lower strike in both of the options. You are, in effect, saying that your original strategy was correct but that the timing was premature. Rolling down will give you the chance to make money at the new price level. This can be a very attractive tactic because it increases the chance of making money and yet you may have been able to make a profit on the original calendar spread after prices have fallen.

If you are looking for lower prices, you could:

> Hold
> Liquidate the position
> Roll down

You may want to hold the position if the time decay in the nearby option is evaporating quickly and you are making more money on the nearby contract than you are losing on the far contract. Holding the position also gives you the possibility of holding the long far contract after the expiration of the near option. However, this tactic should only be used if you expect the price of the underlying to stay within the profit zone.

It may be best to liquidate the position if there is little time decay in the nearby contract and the price is expected to move even farther beyond the estimated break-even points. You may be able to liquidate the trade with a small profit or small loss now rather than wait for a larger loss later.

A final choice is to roll down. You would replace the current strike with a strike at your down-side objective. For example, your original strike could have been at-the-money at 55. Prices may have since dropped to 50, and you expect prices to drop to 45. Rolling down entails liquidating the two options with strikes of 50 and initiating the same calendar spread, but with the strikes at 45. You have, in effect, liquidated a neutral calendar spread in favor of a bearish calendar spread.

If the Price of the Underlying Instrument Rises

If you are looking for higher prices, you could:

> Liquidate the position
> Liquidate the short option

It may be best to liquidate the position if there is little time decay in the nearby option and the price is expected to move even farther beyond the estimated break-even points. You may be able to liquidate the trade with a small profit or small loss now rather than wait for a larger loss later.

A more aggressive tactic is to liquidate the short call. You have then shifted your position to a long call. This means that you will need the market to trade significantly higher before you make a profit on the trade, but you now have much more profit potential.

If you are looking for stable prices, you could:

> Hold if within the expected profit zone
> Liquidate if below expected break-even
> Roll up

You could hold the position if prices have not moved to above your expected break-even at expiration of the first contract.

Alternately, you could liquidate the position if the price of the underlying instrument has fallen above the expected break-even point.

A third choice would be to roll up to a higher strike in both of the options. You are, in effect, saying that your original strategy was correct but the timing was premature. Rolling up will give you the chance to make money at the new price level. This can be a very attractive tactic because it increases the chance of making money and yet you may have been able to make a profit on the original calendar spread after prices have risen.

If you are looking for lower prices, you could:

> Hold the position
> Liquidate the long option

The basic idea behind holding the position is for the price of the underlying instrument to drop back into the profit zone. Usually, you will be holding a slightly unprofitable position if prices have rallied. A drop in price will often bring the calendar spread back into a profitable position.

A more aggressive tactic is to liquidate the long call. You have then shifted your position to a short call. This means that you will likely be making a profit at a higher level than with the calendar spread and will also probably have a greater profit potential for the near term. Another advantage is that you are selling time premium with less time remaining, thus receiving the benefit of the faster time decay that occurs closer to expiration. One disadvantage is that you will be giving up the profit potential of the long call in the long term. In addition, you are taking on more price risk when you carry a naked short call.

16

Ratio Spreads

A. Strategy
B. Equivalent strategy
C. Risk/reward
D. Decision structure

STRATEGY

There are two types of ratio spreads: long and short.

A long ratio spread buys low-strike calls and sells a larger quantity of higher strike calls, or buys high-strike puts and sells a larger quantity of lower strike puts.

A short ratio is the reverse position to the above descriptions. However, it is rare that a short ratio spread will outperform similar strategies. As a result, the rest of the chapter will focus on long ratio spreads. For the rest of the chapter, the term ratio spreads will refer to only long ratio spreads.

Ratio spreads are similar to covered writes. A ratio spread is usually considered neutral strategy, but adjusting the number of short options can change the nature of the spread. The generic ratio spread will have a net delta of zero. Adjusting the number of short options changes the net delta of the position. Assume you want to initiate a ratio spread. Reducing the number of short options to just one converts the ratio spread to a bull spread. A more bearish position can be created by selling enough options to shift the net delta from zero to a negative number.

In general, you are trying to create a delta neutral position. Whenever doing a ratio spread, find the delta of the total position to see if the position is net long or short and if that market exposure fits with your market outlook or strategy.

Ratio spreads are considered neutral strategies because the greatest profit occurs between the selected strike prices. In effect, you are looking for stable price when you initiate a ratio spread. However, note that rolling up or down to keep the price of the underlying instrument between the two strike prices allows you to go with the market if it moves in either direction.

You are trying to make more money on the time premium decay on the short options than you lose on the long option.

One interesting feature of ratio spreads is that they can be initiated with risk in only one price direction. You will only lose money if prices move in the direction of the short options strike.

Let's look at an example of a ratio spread. Assume the following:

S&P 500 = 237.75
December 230 call price = 11.00
December 230 call delta = .69
December 240 call price = 5.50
December 240 call delta = .46

You would construct a delta neutral ratio spread by first finding the ratio between the deltas of the two options. In this case, the ratio of the two options is .69/.46, or 1.5. This means that you will need to short 1.5 of the December 240 calls for every long December 230 call. For example, you will sell 75 December 240 calls if you are long 50 December 230 calls.

EQUIVALENT STRATEGY

Ratio spreads are very similar to ratio covered writes, but there are several differences. The major advantage of a ratio spread is that is has less dollar risk. The major risk in a delta neutral ratio writing or ratio spreading program is that the price of the underlying instrument moves sharply in one direction or another and you are unable to adjust the portfolio to reflect the new net delta of the portfolio. A ratio spread has a built-in safety net with the long call instead of the long underlying instrument. There is no unlimited risk on the down-side because the long call has a limited risk.

Another effect of the use of a long call instead of an underlying instrument is that you can make more money on the down-side. The call's premium will eventually deteriorate if the price declines, yet you will continually be rolling down the short options as the price declines. Your position will become increasingly delta short even though you haven't increased your risk relative to the initial price level. This is because the position would be delta neutral again if the price rallied back to the initial level. The net effect is that you can make more money on the down-side than on the up-side by simply leaving the original long call intact.

The disadvantage of the ratio spread versus the ratio write is that you are buying time premium when you buy the long call. One of the major objects of ratio writing and spreading is to capture the time decay in the short options. A ratio spread counteracts much of that gain by being long a call with its own decaying time premium.

RISK/REWARD

Maximum Profit

The maximum profit equals the number of long calls or puts multiplied by the difference between the strikes, plus the initial credit (if initiated for a credit) or minus the initial debit (if initiated for a debit). This rather complicated formula can be easily grasped with the help of an example. Assume the following situation:

> Squib = 103
> January 100 calls = 8 1/2
> January 105 calls = 6 3/8

You are quite bearish and sell three January 105 calls and buy only one January 100 call. The net credit on the trade is 10 5/8. The maximum profit, assuming no followup action, is the number of long calls, 1, times the difference in strike prices, 5, to equal 5. Then add the net credit, 10 5/8, for a total of 15 5/8.

Break-even Point

For a call ratio spread, the up-side break-even point equals the high strike price plus (the maximum profit divided by the number of naked options).

For a put ratio spread, the down-side break-even point equals the low strike price minus (the maximum profit divided by the number of naked options).

Remember that these formulas only apply to a ratio spread that you do not adjust after entry. Nonetheless, let's look at an example. Assume the same situation as above. Your maximum profit was 15 5/8. This means that the up-side break-even can be calculated by first dividing the maximum profit, 15 5/8, by the number of naked options, 2, for 7 13/16. Add this to the high strike price, 105, making the up-side break-even point 112 13/16.

Risk

If the trade is put on for a credit, there is no risk in one price direction, the direction of the short option. At expiration, the short options will be losing dollar for dollar with the underlying for each naked short option.

If the trade is initiated for a debit, the risk is the debit in the direction of the long option plus the same risk mentioned above in the direction of the short option.

DECISION STRUCTURE

Selection

The first decision is your market stance. Generally, ratio spreads are neutral strategies, though you can adjust the market stance by adjusting the ratio and by adjusting the strike prices.

For example, using calls, the more short calls you write, the more bearish the position. The lower the strike prices, the more bearish the position.

A major question is whether you require this trade to be done at a credit or whether you will accept a debit spread.

It would be useful to examine the chapters on ratio covered writing (Chapter 8 - Ratio Covered Call Writing and Chapter 11 - Ratio Covered Put Writing) for further details on the implications of a delta neutral strategy.

As a general rule, you should be striving to buy intrinsic value and selling time value. This suggests that you should generally be buying far in-the-money options and selling at-the-money or slightly out-of-the-money options.

Follow-up actions

Ratio spreads can be initiated as bull or bear strategies or as a delta neutral strategy. The first section below outlines the follow-up action for a delta neutral strategy and the following two sections outline the follow-up actions for bull or bear ratio spreads.

If the Price of the Underlying Instrument Moves Significantly While a Delta Neutral Position Is Held

Basically, you will be trying to keep the position as delta neutral as possible throughout the life of the trade. This will theoretically eliminate price risk as a consideration. In addition, it should maximize the amount of time premium that is captured. The tricky task is to keep the trade delta neutral. The problem is that the deltas of the options change as the price of the underlying instrument changes. If the price of the underlying instrument climbs, the delta of the short options increases more than the delta of the long options, thus making you increasingly short. A declining underlying instrument will make your position increasingly long. You therefore must continually adjust the ratio of the long to short options.

For example, you are long 100 options on the S&P 500 futures contract with a strike of 230 and a delta of .69, and short 150 contracts of the S&P 500 options with a strike of 240 and a delta of .46. The current price of the futures contract is 237.75. If the price of the S&P 500 climbs to 243, the delta of the options will climb to, say,

.79 and .58, respectively. Thus, you will be the equivalent of short eight contracts of the futures. This can be found by multiplying the delta of the long option, .79, by the number of long options, 100, and subtracting the number of short options, 150 times the delta, .58: ((.79 X 100) - (.58 X 150) = -8). You will now be exposed to risk if the market continues higher.

You must therefore adjust the number of contracts you are using to reduce the net delta of the position to zero. To find the new quantity of options, divide the net delta of the long side, in this example, 79 (a delta of .79 X 100, the number of long options, = 79), by the new delta, .58. The result, 136.2, will have to be rounded to 136. You should then liquidate 14 of your short options to bring your portfolio to the proper weighting of 136.

Note that you will have to resell those 14 contracts if the price of the underlying instrument drops back down to 237.75. In addition, a further drop in price would require you to sell additional contracts.

It should be clear that ratio spreading requires active management. You simply cannot go away for a vacation and expect to still have a delta neutral position. Note also that the more the price moves in one direction the more the delta is moving against you.

A second adjustment should also be made to the position after the price of the underlying instrument has moved. Remember, the point of the trade is to capture time premium. Therefore, you should roll up or down as the price of the underlying instrument moves from the initial strike price to another strike price. For example, if the price of the S&P 500 futures moves from 240 to 250, you should buy back your 240 calls and sell 250 calls. Conversely, if the price of the underlying should drop to a lower strike price, you should roll down out of your current strike price and into the new at-the-money option.

There are two major problems with a ratio spreading program.

First, how often should the portfolio be rebalanced? Theoretically, you should rebalance every time there is a price change that implies a change of one contract in the short call position. The trade-off is that continual adjusting may create too many commissions. This will occur if the price of the underlying instrument jumps back and forth in a narrow range. You will be adjusting your short call portfolio with every jump in the price of the underlying instrument, creating commission expense, yet the price of the underlying instrument won't really break out of its range.

Unfortunately, there is little that can be done about this except to not adjust the portfolio as often as would be suggested by keeping the trade delta neutral. The risk of this tactic is that the market will move enough in one direction to create a market exposure and you lose money because of this exposure.

In the final analysis, it is probably better to adjust whenever necessary and pay the extra commissions as the cost of not exposing yourself to market risk.

If the Price of the Underlying Instrument Rises

Ratio Call Spreads

If you expect prices to move higher, you could:

> Liquidate the short options
> Liquidate
> Roll up

The most aggressive approach would be to liquidate the short options. This would shift the position to a net long call position. Hopefully, you are adjusting the position because of newfound bullishness, not because you lost money due to a poor adjustment to the ratio because of the higher prices. If you are adjusting because you are now bullish, you may have a slight profit in the trade because of the decay in the time premium. Thus, you will be shifting to a long call position with a profit that, in effect, raises the break-even point. One problem with this tactic is that you likely initiated the original ratio spread with little time left before expiration. This means that you will be buying time premium when time is working significantly against you.

A more conservative and probably the most flexible approach is to liquidate the position. You will then be able to select from a larger variety of bullish positions to take.

If you have a bullish ratio spread, you may want to roll up. This will maximize your profits if you roll up every time the short options hit another strike price. You will then be writing more time premium while keeping your long option largely composed of intrinsic value. The same tactic should not be used for a bearish ratio spread because you should never use a bearish strategy when you are bullish.

If you expect prices to remain about the same, you could:

> Hold if profitable
> Roll up if unprofitable

If the position is profitable, you are likely holding a bullish ratio spread, and holding the position can make sense. Holding the position will mainly accomplish the goal of capturing the time premium on the short options.

If the position is unprofitable, you are likely holding a bearish ratio spread and rolling up to higher strike prices may help recover some of the losses. This is basically a tactic to try to maximize the time premium that you capture. Thus, the short options should be at-the-money while the long options should be in-the-money.

If you expect prices to move lower, you could:

> Hold
> Sell more calls

If you are holding a bearish ratio spread, then holding the position makes sense. You have the right strategy, but you have initiated the trade at too low a price. A slide in prices will put the trade back on a firm footing.

A more aggressive approach would be to sell more calls or liquidate some long calls. The ultimate version of this tactic is to liquidate all the long calls. You have to be very confident of your bearish prognostication because of the greater risk of a naked short call position. However, the potential reward is also much higher.

Ratio Put Spreads

If you expect prices to move higher, you could:

> Hold if initiated at a credit
> Liquidate the long option
> Roll up

If you were able to initiate the ratio put spread at a credit, you can hold the position. You have no up-side risk in a ratio put spread if initiated for a credit. As a result, you should continue to hold the position. Holding the position will give you additional time for prices to move back to the maximum profit point.

The most aggressive choice is to liquidate the long put and simply carry the short puts. This will create large profits if prices move higher, but will bring very large losses if prices change direction and fall.

A more moderate alternative is to roll up. If the position is profitable, you are likely holding a bullish ratio spread. Rolling up to higher strike prices will maximize the time premium that you capture. Make sure the short option is at-the-money while the long option is in-the-money.

If you expect prices to remain about the same, you could:

> Hold if profitable
> Roll up if unprofitable

If the position is profitable, you are likely holding a bullish ratio spread and holding the position can make sense. Holding the position will mainly accomplish the goal of capturing the time premium on the short options.

If the position is unprofitable, you are likely holding a bearish ratio spread and rolling up to higher strike prices may help recover some of the losses. This is basically a tactic to try to maximize the time premium that you capture. Thus, the short options should be at-the-money while the long option should be in-the-money.

If you expect prices to move lower, you could:

> Hold the position
> Buy more puts

If you are holding a bearish ratio spread, then holding the position makes sense. You have the right strategy, but you have initiated the trade at too low a price. A slide in prices will likely add to your profits.

A more aggressive approach would be to sell more puts or liquidate some of your short puts. The ultimate version of this tactic would be to liquidate all the short puts. You would have to be very confident of your bearish prognostication because of the somewhat greater risk of a long put position. However, the potential reward is also much higher.

If the Price of the Underlying Instrument Drops

Ratio Call Spreads

If you expect prices to move higher, you could:

> Hold the position
> Liquidate
> Liquidate the short options or buy more calls

If you have a bullish ratio call spread, then holding the position makes sense. The price of the underlying has moved lower but you are now looking for the market to move in your direction. Your position should therefore begin to show a profit if your market opinion is correct. On the other hand, you will not want to hold the position if you have a bearish ratio spread.

If you initiated a bearish ratio spread, then you should consider liquidating the position. There is never any reason to hold a bearish position if you are bullish.

The most aggressive approach would be to liquidate the short options or buy more calls. This would shift the position to a net long call position. Hopefully, you are adjusting the position because of new-found bullishness, not because you lost money due to a poor adjustment to the ratio because of the higher prices. If you are adjusting because you are now bullish, you may have a slight profit in the trade because of the decay in the time premium. Thus, you will be shifting to a long call position with a profit that, in effect, raises the break-even point. One problem with this tactic is that you likely initiated the original ratio spread with little time left before expiration. This means that you will be buying time premium when time is working significantly against you.

If you expect prices to remain about the same, you could:

> Hold if profitable
> Roll down if unprofitable

If the position is profitable, you are likely holding a bearish ratio spread and holding the position can make sense. Holding the position will mainly accomplish the goal of capturing the time premium on the short options.

If the position is unprofitable, you are likely holding a bullish ratio spread and rolling down to lower strike prices may help recover some of the losses. This is basically a tactic to try to maximize the time premium that you capture. Thus, the short options should be at-the-money while the long option should be in-the-money.

If you expect prices to move lower, you could:

> Hold if initiated at a credit
> Roll down
> Liquidate the long calls or sell more calls

If you are holding a bearish ratio spread, then holding the position makes sense. An expectation of lower prices will lead to greater profits. No matter what market bias you have, consider holding the position whenever you have initiated the trade for a credit.

If the position is unprofitable, you are likely holding a bullish ratio spread and rolling down to lower strike prices may help recover some of the losses. This is basically a tactic to try to maximize the time premium that you capture. Thus, the short options should be at-the-money while the long option should be in-the-money.

A more aggressive approach is to sell more calls or liquidate some long calls. The ultimate version of this tactic is to liquidate all the long calls. You have to be very confident of your bearish prognostication because of the greater risk of a naked short call position. However, the potential reward is also much higher.

Ratio Put Spreads

If you expect prices to move higher, you could:

> Hold if initiated at a credit
> Liquidate the long puts or sell more puts

If you were able to initiate the ratio put spread at a credit then you can hold the position. You have no up-side risk in a ratio put spread if initiated for a credit. As a result, you should continue to hold the position. If you have a bullish ratio put spread, then holding the position will give you additional time for prices to move back to the maximum profit point.

The most aggressive choice is to liquidate the long puts or add to the short puts. This will bring large profits if prices move higher, but will have very large losses if prices change direction and fall. You must have a firm opinion about the expected rally.

If you expect prices to remain about the same, you could:

> Hold if profitable
> Roll down if unprofitable

If the position is profitable, you are likely holding a bearish ratio spread and holding the position can make sense. Holding the position will mainly accomplish the goal of capturing the time premium on the short options.

If the position is unprofitable, you are likely holding a bullish ratio spread. Rolling down to lower strike prices may help recover some of the losses. This is basically a tactic to try to maximize the time premium that you capture. Thus, the short options should be at-the-money while the long options should be in-the-money.

If you expect prices to move lower, you could:

> Hold the position
> Liquidate the position
> Buy more puts or liquidate the short puts
> Roll down

If the position is profitable, you are likely holding a bearish ratio spread, and holding the position can make sense. Holding the position will mainly accomplish the goal of capturing the time premium on the short options.

If you are holding a bullish position, then the most flexible approach is to liquidate the position. You will then be able to select from a larger variety of bearish positions to take.

A more aggressive approach would be to buy more puts or liquidate some of your short puts. The ultimate version of this tactic would be to liquidate all the short puts. You would have to be very confident of your bearish prognostication because of the somewhat greater risk of a long put position. However, the potential reward is also much higher.

If the position is unprofitable, you are likely holding a bullish ratio spread and rolling down to lower strike prices may help recover some of the losses. This is basically a tactic to try to maximize the time premium that you capture. Thus, the short options should be at-the-money while the long option should be in-the-money.

17

Ratio Calendar Spreads

A. Strategy
B. Risk/reward
C. Decision structure

STRATEGY

The ratio calendar spread is a blending of ratio and calendar spreads. It consists of selling nearby options and buying fewer of a farther option. For example, you could sell 4 of the July 40 calls and buy 2 of the October 40 calls.

The amount of bullishness or bearishness can be controlled by the ratio of the long and short options. A neutral spread can be constructed as a delta neutral strategy, and then kept neutral throughout the time period. Alternately, positions can be engineered that have a bullish or bearish bias.

Ratio calendar spreads are good low-risk investments that can give a steady return. They capture the higher time decay of the nearby option but maintain the hedge of the far option. In addition, ratio calendar spreads have the potential for large gains after the nearby option expires because of the still-existing long-term option. For more information, see Chapter 15 - Calendar Spreads and Chapter 16 - Ratio Spreads.

RISK/REWARD

Unfortunately, we cannot present formulas to identify the risk and rewards of ratio calendar spreads. The strategy is too dynamic to reduce to formulas. Much of the profits or losses are related to time decay of two different options. Thus, concepts such as break-evens are changing all the time. However, profits and losses can be estimated using a computer program that simulates time decay. The ramifications of time decay are addressed in Chapter 15 - Calendar Spreads.

DECISION STRUCTURE

Selection

First, determine your overall strategy. There are two major strategies with ratio calendar spreads: market bias or delta neutral.

The first attempts to construct a ratio calendar spread that will profit through changes in the price of the underlying instrument by adjusting the various strike prices and ratios of near to far options. The second looks mainly to capture the time premium of the nearby option but to retain the possibility of large capital gains after the nearby option expires.

If you have a market bias, use the deltas of the various options to determine the correct market exposure. Select a strike price that corresponds with your expected price scenario. Preferably, you will initiate the trade at a credit. This will ensure a profit even if prices don't move. However, there is a trade-off. In general, a large credit will occur only if you have shorted a relatively large number of options relative to the long side. The greater the ratio, the greater price risk if the position goes against you.

For a delta neutral strategy, set up the initial position with the total delta of the nearby option position equal to the total delta of the far option. A main object of this trade is to capture the time premium of the nearby option. You should therefore be writing the at-the-money option. Preferably, you will also be selling an option with a high implied volatility and buying one with a low implied volatility.

If the Price of the Underlying Instrument Changes Significantly

With the delta neutral strategy, you will adjust the longs and shorts to maintain delta neutrality. In addition, you can roll up or down to new strikes if the transaction costs are not prohibitive (i.e. net gain in selling time premium is greater than transaction costs).

With a market bias strategy, you may want to liquidate the trade if the price of the underlying instrument moves through the estimated eventual break-even point before the expiration of the nearby contract. Assume you have a 2:1 ratio in July and October options. Your ideal scenario would be a drop in price to below the strike price, with the nearby option expiring worthless, and then the underlying instrument price moving strongly higher.

However, the price may move higher before the July expiration, necessitating a defensive liquidation. Note how important your market outlook is. You should definitely liquidate the position if you look for prices to continue higher before expiration. A bearish outlook suggests that you hold the original position.

Once again, an examination of Chapter 15 - Calendar Spreads and Chapter 16 - Ratio Spreads will be helpful in understanding the potential follow-up tactics.

18

Straddles

STRATEGY

There are two types of straddles: long and short. They are constructed as follows:

Long straddle = long call and long put
Short straddle = short call and short put

Straddles are generally considered neutral strategies because the put and call are usually both at-the-money options. This means that the long straddle will profit if the price of the underlying instrument moves significantly in one direction or the other. The short straddle will profit if the price of the underlying instrument stays in a narrow range.

A combination is a straddle but with the terms of the put and call different. For example, a straddle is long the December 50 call and the December 50 put. A combination would be long the December 50 call and short the December 60 put.

Note also that bullish and bearish straddles can be constructed. For example, a bullish long straddle would have the strike prices below the current price of the underlying instrument, thus maximizing the profits on the bull side but increasing the chances of losses if prices move lower. A bullish short straddle would be constructed by selecting strike prices above the current price of the underlying instrument. Prices would have to rise to within the two break-even points before you would profit.

Long straddles are always initiated for a debit, while short straddles are always initiated at a credit.

RISK/REWARD

Maximum Profit

Long Straddle   Maximum profit is unlimited. Once one of the break-even points is breached, the profit will be equal, dollar for dollar, the amount that the underlying instrument is above or below the break-even at expiration. Thus, you will want the price of the underlying instrument to trend strongly in one direction.

Short Straddle   Maximum profit is the net credit. This will occur at the strike price. Thus, you will want the price of the underlying instrument to stagnate near the strike price of the straddle.

Break-even Point

The break-even points of long and short straddles are calculated essentially the same way.

> ### Long Straddles
> Up-side break-even = strike price + net debit
> Down-side break-even = strike price - net debit

> ### Short Straddles
> Up-side break-even = strike price + net credit
> Down-side break-even = strike price - net credit

Let's look at a couple of examples. Suppose you initiated a long straddle using options on Textron for December expiration. Textron is trading at 59 3/4, so you buy the 60 call and the 60 put for 3 each. The net debit is $6, thus making your break-even points $66 and $54. The up-side break-even is equal to the strike price, $60, plus the net debit, $6, for a total of $66. The down-side break-even is equal to the strike price, $60, minus the net debit, $6, for a total of $54.

Assume the following prices:

> Intel = 20 1/4
> November 20 call = 1 1/4
> November 20 put = 1 1/4
> Net credit = 2 1/2

The up-side break-even on a short straddle is the strike price, 20, plus the net credit, 2 1/2, for a total of 22 1/2. The down-side break-even is the strike price, 20, minus the net credit, 2 1/2, for a total of 17 1/2.

Maximum Risk

A long straddle has a limited risk of just the debit paid for the straddle. No further losses can occur. The maximum risk occurs at the strike price of the straddle.

The dollar risk on a short straddle is unlimited. Once the price of the underlying instruments breaches the break-even points, the loss will be dollar for dollar the amount that the price of the underlying instrument is above or below the break-even at expiration.

DECISION STRUCTURE

Selection

Long Straddle

You are looking for more price movement than the market expects. The main problem with straddles is that there is a tendency for the most volatile instruments to have the most expensive straddles. In effect, you should compare the price range suggested by the implied volatility with your expected price range.

A second way to look at the straddle is to apply the criteria for a call purchase and a put purchase simultaneously. However, it will be rare to find a situation that has both legs attractively priced.

Short Straddle

The short straddle is the reverse situation. You are looking for a situation where the market has implied a greater volatility than you expected, or where both the put and the call are unattractively priced.

If the Price of the Underlying Instrument Drops

Long Straddle

If you expect prices to move higher, you could:

> Hold the position
> Liquidate the position
> Liquidate the put

You should only hold the position if you look for the price of the underlying instrument to surmount the up-side break-even point. This will usually be less likely now that prices are at a lower level.

You may be able to liquidate the position for a profit at the lower level. This will likely occur when the option is about to expire. It makes sense to liquidate now rather than risk a move back up to above the down-side break-even point.

The most bullish strategy would be to liquidate the put and stick with the long call. The net effect is that you are taking a bullish stance on the market and believe that there is no further possibility of profit on the down-side. You are, in effect, initiating a new trade at the current price level. You are increasing the profit potential by decreasing the cost of the position relative to a straddle, but you are also decreasing the chances of success.

If you expect prices to remain stable, you could:

> Hold if profitable
> Liquidate the position

You should only hold the position if you are carrying a profitable position. This means that you should now expect the price of the underlying instrument to stabilize below the down-side break-even point.

You may be able to liquidate the position for a profit at the lower level. This will likely occur when the option is about to expire. It makes sense to liquidate now rather than risk a move back up to above the down-side break-even point. It also makes sense to liquidate the position if prices are expected to stabilize above the down-side break-even point. The loss will be less if the position is liquidated early than if you had waited for expiration.

If you expect prices to move lower, you could:

> Hold the position
> Liquidate the call

You should definitely hold the position if you look for lower prices. Your game plan is working and the profits should continue to mount.

A more aggressive position would be to liquidate the call. This will give you a long put in a declining market. Your risk will be slightly higher because you will not have the hedge of the long call to protect you against a sharp rally. Your profits will be higher than holding the original spread because you will have liquidated the call while it still had some premium left.

Short Straddle

If you expect prices to move higher, you could:

> Hold the position
> Liquidate the position
> Liquidate the call

You should definitely hold the position if you look for higher prices. The success of the short straddle is dependent on prices being within the two break-even points at expiration. With prices now lower than when you initiated the spread, you need a rally to help your position.

You may be able to liquidate the position for a profit if prices are still within the break-even points. It makes sense to liquidate now rather than risk a move to below the down-side break-even point.

The most bullish strategy would be to liquidate the call and stick with the short put. The net effect is that you are taking a bullish stance on the market and believe that there is no further possibility of profit on the down-side. You are, in effect, initiating a new trade at the current price level. You are increasing the profit potential by decreasing the cost of the position relative to a straddle, but you are also decreasing the chances of success.

If you expect prices to remain stable, you could:

> Hold if profitable
> Liquidate if unprofitable

You should definitely hold the position if you have profits in the position. The success of the short straddle is dependent on the price being within the two break-even points at expiration. If you have a profit on the trade, then prices are likely to be within the two break-even points. Stable price action will help you because you are selling time premium and your profits should mount as time passes.

You may be able to liquidate the position for a profit if prices are still within the break-even points. It makes sense to liquidate now rather than risk a move to below the down-side break-even point. If the position is currently unprofitable, you are probably on the outside of the break-even points. Liquidating the trade now may limit your losses to a small amount rather that running the risk of a larger loss later.

If you expect prices to move lower, you could:

> Liquidate the position
> Liquidate the call

You should liquidate the position if you look for lower prices. You will lose more money if the price of the underlying instrument moves lower. It is therefore imperative that you take a defensive action to minimize losses.

Liquidating the put is a more bearish approach. You are now saying that the market is not neutral but bearish, and you want to jump on the bandwagon. Shifting to a naked short call will keep you on the side of writing time premium but also keep you exposed to risk if the price of the underlying instrument rallies sharply.

If the Price of the Underlying Instrument Rises

Long Straddle

If you expect prices to move higher, you could:

> Hold the position
> Liquidate the position
> Liquidate put

You should definitely hold the position if you look for higher prices. Your game plan is working and the profits should continue to mount.

You may be able to liquidate the position for a profit at the higher level. This will likely occur when the option is about to expire. It makes sense to liquidate now rather than risk a move back down to below the up-side break-even point.

The most bullish strategy would be to liquidate the put and stick with the long call. The net effect is that you are taking a bullish stance on the market and believe that there is no further possibility of profit on the down-side. You are, in effect, initiating a new trade at the current price level. You are increasing the profit potential by decreasing the cost of the position relative to a straddle, but you are also decreasing the chances of success.

If you expect prices to remain stable, you could:

> Hold if profitable
> Liquidate the position

You should only hold the position if you are carrying a profitable position. This means that you should now expect the price of the underlying instrument to stabilize above the up-side break-even point.

You may be able to liquidate the position for a profit at the higher level. This will likely occur when the option is about to expire. It makes sense to liquidate now rather than risk a move down to below the up-side break-even point. It also makes sense to liquidate the position if prices are expected to stabilize below the up-side break-even point. The loss will be less if the position is liquidated early than if you wait for expiration.

If you expect prices to move lower, you could:

> Liquidate the position
> Liquidate the call

You may be able to liquidate the position for a profit if prices are outside the break-even points. It makes sense to liquidate now rather than risk a move to below the up-side break-even point.

A more aggressive position would be to liquidate the call. This will give you a long put in a declining market. Your risk will be slightly higher because you will not have the hedge of the long call to protect you against a sharp rally. This is a risky tactic because you are calling for the market to change trend. Nonetheless, your potential profits will be higher than holding the original spread because you will have liquidated the call while it had a lot of premium.

Short Straddle

If you expect prices to move higher, you could:

> Liquidate the position
> Liquidate the call

You may be able to liquidate the position for a profit if prices are still within the break-even points. It makes sense to liquidate now rather than risk a move to below the down-side break-even point.

The most aggressive approach is to liquidate the call. This will leave you with a short put. The put will likely be out-of-the-money, so the risk of losing money on the put should be minimal. By the same token, your profit potential is limited to the remaining time premium, which is likely to be very little.

If you expect prices to remain stable, you could:

> Hold if profitable
> Liquidate if unprofitable

You should definitely hold the position if you have profits in the position. The success of the short straddle is dependent on the price being within the two break-even points at expiration. If you have a profit on the trade, then prices are likely to be within the two break-even points. Stable price action will help you because you are selling time premium. Your profits should mount as time passes.

You may be able to liquidate the position for a profit if prices are still within the break-even points. It makes sense to liquidate now rather than risk a move to above the up-side break-even point. If the position is currently unprofitable, you are probably on the outside of the break-even points. Liquidating the trade now may limit your losses to a small amount rather that running the risk of a larger loss later.

If you expect prices to move lower, you could:

> Hold the position
> Liquidate the put

You should definitely hold the position if you look for lower prices. The success of the short straddle is dependent on the price being within the two break-even points at expiration. With prices now higher than when you initiated the spread, you need a price drop to help your position.

Liquidating the put is a more bearish approach. You are now saying that the market is not neutral but bearish, and you want to jump on the bandwagon. Shifting to a naked short call will keep you on the side of writing time premium, but it will also keep you exposed to risk if the price of the underlying instrument rallies sharply.

19

Synthetic Calls
and Puts

A. Strategy
B. Equivalent strategy
C. Risk/reward
D. Decision structure

STRATEGY

A synthetic call can be created by buying a put and buying the underlying instrument. A synthetic put can be created by buying a call and shorting the underlying instrument.

There is no reason to initiate a synthetic put or call if an exchange or OTC option exists. A synthetic put or call costs more because of the extra commissions.

On the other hand, it is possible that you have sold short the underlying instrument, but decide later to limit your risk by buying a call. It may also make sense to buy a call to lock in a profit on your short sale but still allow you some profit potential. Alternately, you might have bought a call, turned bearish, and decided to short the underlying instrument. The same kind of situation may exist for buying the underlying instrument and later buying a put to limit your risk or help lock in a profit.

Generally, all of the ramifications of a synthetic put or call are the same as for a regular put or call. We will therefore confine our remarks to the differences between synthetic and regular options. (See Chapter 4 - Buy A Call and Chapter 5 - Buy A Put for more details.)

EQUIVALENT STRATEGY

An equivalent strategy would be to buy a put or call. As stated above, buying a regular option will be less expensive than initiating a synthetic option. In addition, the regular option will likely have greater liquidity.

RISK/REWARD

Maximum Risk

The maximum risk of a synthetic option is the maximum amount of money that can be lost. Note that this is essentially the premium of the put. The maximum risk of holding a regular option is equal to the premium; the same can be said of the synthetic option.

Let's look at the synthetic put as an example. The maximum risk, or premium, is equal to the call strike price minus the price of the underlying instrument plus the price of the call. For example, you buy an OEX 150 call at 5 when the underlying index is at 140. The premium is 10 (150 - 145 + 5 = 10). Thus, the maximum risk of the synthetic put is 10 points.

Break-even Point

Once again, let's look at the synthetic put as an example. The break-even point is equal to the price of the underlying instrument minus the premium of the synthetic put. In the above example, the underlying index will have to trade down to 135 before you split even (145 - 10 = 135). The break-even point for the synthetic call is the price of the underlying instrument plus the premium of the synthetic call.

DECISION STRUCTURE

Selection

The key for this trade is the selection of the exchange-traded option's strike price. For example, selecting an in-the-money call when creating a synthetic put will give greater protection to the short sale while selecting an out-of-the-money call will give the greatest profit potential.

If the Price of the Underlying Instrument Drops

The analysis of the follow-up actions for synthetic options is the same for both the synthetic put and the synthetic call. The discussion below will focus on the synthetic put, but you merely have to flip the discussion over to apply to synthetic calls.

If you expect prices to rally, you could liquidate the short sale and retain the call. You will now be holding just the call, and will not have the bearish protection and down-side profit potential that the short sale gave you. This strategy is risky because it forces you to call a bottom in the market. In addition, you may not be holding the proper call given your market outlook. Now that you are bullish, you may prefer to have a more in-the-money call than the one used in your synthetic put.

A second alternative is to liquidate both sides of the trade and take your profits to the bank. You can structure a new trade to take advantage of your bullish approach rather than trying to shoehorn your existing call into your market outlook.

On the other hand, if you are looking for the market to drop further, you have four choices.

First, you could liquidate the call. Liquidating the call will give you a more aggressive posture on the short side because it will leave you without the protection of the call. The advantage is that you no longer have the cost of the protection, the call premium, to reduce your profits.

A second choice is to roll up to a higher strike price for the call. This will reduce the cost of your protection because you will be substituting a lower priced call for a higher priced call. The net effect is that you are increasing your profit potential while decreasing your protection. One positive aspect is that you will be able to take some profits home with you from rolling up to the lower priced call. A major consideration with this strategy is that there may not be as much liquidity as you need to initiate a position in the higher strike call.

The third choice is to roll down to gain more protection. In effect, you are trying to lock in a profit by rolling down. Note, however, that this strategy will cost you additional outlays because you are substituting a lower strike call for a higher strike call. This strategy should only be attractive if you are becoming less sure of the future direction, or if you think there is little profit potential in the downside.

The final choice is to leave your current position on. This retains the protection and profit potential you originally desired and requires no additional capital outlay.

If the Underlying Instrument Rises

You have three choices if you are looking for continued higher prices.

The first choice is to liquidate the trade. This will be the usual reaction to a money-losing position. The question really is whether or not the additional dollar risk is worth the chance that prices will move lower. The higher the remaining premium the more sense it makes to liquidate the trade and limit your losses.

The second choice is to liquidate the short position but retain the call. This is the most bullish of the choices. You will now have the greatest profit potential but the least protection. The protection of the call has been eliminated.

The third choice is to roll down into a more protective call. Rolling down to a lower strike price will give greater protection because it will have a greater premium. The unfortunate side is that the profit potential will be less.

If the Option Is About to Expire

You can roll the option forward into the next expiration month, using the same criteria used above. In other words, you will know if the underlying instrument will have dropped by the time you have to roll forward. Your decision then becomes what to do with the position. Refer to the two preceding sections to trace through the logical process.

20

Synthetic Longs
and Shorts

A. Strategy
B. Equivalent strategy
C. Risk/reward
D. Decision structure

STRATEGY

It is possible to create synthetic long or short positions in the underlying instrument through various combinations of options. A conversion is a synthetic long position. A reverse conversion is a synthetic short position, often called a reversal.

A conversion is formed by buying a put and selling a call. A reversal is formed by buying a call and selling a put.

Conversions and reversals are constructed to serve basically two objectives:

     1. To create synthetic long or short positions that mimic the price action of the underlying instrument.
     2. To arbitrage versus the opposite position in the underlying instrument.

Another way of looking at conversions or reversals is that they are essentially futures contracts on the underlying instrument. That is, they represent the market's estimate of the future value of the underlying instrument. As such, conversions and reversals can be used in the same ways that futures contracts can be used. An example is to use the reversal to hedge a long position in a common stock.

EQUIVALENT STRATEGY

Buying the underlying instrument is similar to a conversion; shorting the instrument is similar to a reverse conversion. There will be a big difference between the two strategies only if the underlying instrument pays dividends or interest. For example, you will have to pay dividends if you are short stock but not if you have a reversal.

There is no equivalent strategy to the arbitrage.

RISK/REWARD

Conversions or reversals as substitutes for long or short positions have identical risk/reward profiles to their nonsynthetic brethren.

The rest of the this section will deal exclusively with the use of conversions and reversals in arbitrage.

Maximum Profit

Conversion

The simple maximum profit equals the strike price plus the call price minus the put price minus the price of the underlying instrument.

However, carrying charges are important when discussing conversions unless you will not be using margin, or unless the underlying instrument does not pay dividends or interest. They will have a major impact on the profitability of the trade.

Note that you have locked in a profit at the outset of the trade. Presumably, your only concerns after entry will be unanticipated changes in the carrying charges. For example, there may be a cut in dividends or a rise in financing costs.

Reversal

The simple maximum profit equals the price of the underlying instrument plus the price of the put minus the price of the call minus the strike price.

The carrying charges are also critical in calculating the maximum profit potential. A reversal requires the payment of dividends or interest payments.

Break-even Point

As a trade, there is no break-even. Subsequent price action is irrelevant to the outcome of the arbitrage.

However, change in carrying charges will affect the outcome of the arbitrage, and a break-even point could be identified for each of the components of the carrying charges. For example, you will make money if the dividend payout stays at 5 percent, but you will lose money if the dividend moves below 2.5 percent. Thus, 2.5 percent on the annualized dividend yield becomes your break-even point.

Maximum Risk

The maximum risk for an arbitrage will not be related to price but to changes in the carrying charges. As was mentioned above, the carrying charges are working for you or against you. They become the major determinant of profitability once you are in the trade.

The only outside risk is the risk of assignment on the short option. As the short option moves further into the money, you may want to try to roll strikes closer to the at-the-money options.

DECISION STRUCTURE

There is no decision structure that is similar to that of the other strategies in this book. Instead, the decision structure is very simple.

You will initiate an arbitrage only if the difference in price between the actual instrument plus the net carrying charges minus transaction costs equals a profit. Once again, the key to the arbitrage is the carrying charges. They must be calculated accurately and monitored closely.

There is no follow-up action to take unless the carrying charges are changing against you. At that time you should liquidate the trade to limit losses.

21

For Further
Information

You may receive a free copy of the decision structure of each of the strategies outlined in this book by writing to the author at:

> Courtney D. Smith
> 675 West Hastings, #1614
> Vancouver, B.C. V6R 4W3
> Canada

There are also several other good books on options that emphasize other aspects of options.

The Stock Options Manual (McGraw-Hill, 1979) by Gary Gastineau presents much of the basics of options and has a good overview of options pricing theories.

Options Pricing (Dow Jones-Irwin, 1983) by Robert A. Jarrow and Andrew Rudd takes a much deeper look at option pricing. The math is intense but worth it for those who can understand it.

Complete Guide To Commodity Options (John Wiley & Sons, 1985) by John Labuzcewski and Jeanne Sinquefield is an excellent guide to commodity options. Of particular interest is the use of options for hedging purposes. Many of the concepts can be applied to instruments other than futures.

Index